JAKE BAILEY | WHAT CANCER TAUGHT ME

JAKE BAILEY

WHAT CANCER TAUGHT ME

BAILEY

WITH NICOLA McCLOY

PENGUIN BOOKS

ABOUT THE AUTHOR

Teenager Jake Bailey grabbed headlines around the world when he delivered a rousing speech from a wheelchair at his school's end-of-year prizegiving in 2015. At the time Jake was head boy at Christchurch Boys' High School, and had just one week earlier been diagnosed with the fastest growing form of cancer, Burkitt's non-Hodgkin's lymphoma. He was given two weeks to live if the cancer was left untreated, and was hospitalised for three months while undergoing intensive chemotherapy treatment.

A video of the speech that Jake made to his fellow students was viewed by millions and attracted media attention globally. His now famous quote — 'Here's the thing, none of us get out of life alive, so be gallant, be great, be gracious, and be grateful for the opportunities you have' — was voted Massey University's 2015 New Zealand Quote of the Year.

Now in remission, Jake is based on the Gold Coast in Australia, from where he travels to deliver inspirational speeches that draw on his experience of cancer and all that it has taught him. He is an ambassador for the Māia Health Foundation in New Zealand and the Tour de Cure in Australia.

PENGUIN

UK | USA | Canada | Ireland | Australia
India | New Zealand | South Africa | China

Penguin is an imprint of the Penguin Random House group of companies,
whose addresses can be found at global.penguinrandomhouse.com.

Penguin
Random House
New Zealand

First published by Penguin Random House New Zealand, 2017

1 3 5 7 9 10 8 6 4 2

Text © Jake Bailey, 2017

The right of Nicola McCloy to be identified as the author of this work in
terms of section 96 of the Copyright Act 1994 is hereby asserted.

Cover design by Emma Jakicevich © Penguin Random House New Zealand
Text design by Kate Barraclough © Penguin Random House New Zealand
Cover photograph by Stephen Goodenough
Prepress by Image Centre Group
Printed and bound in Australia by Griffin Press, an Accredited ISO AS/NZS
14001 Environmental Management Systems Printer

A catalogue record for this book is available from
the National Library of New Zealand.

ISBN 978-0-14-377086-2
eISBN 978-0-14-377087-9

penguin.co.nz

For the staff of the Christchurch BMTU and my haematologist, without whom I wouldn't be here to write this, and the nurse without whom my speech would never have happened.

CONTENTS

It is not the critic who counts; not the man who points out how the strong man stumbles, or where the doer of deeds could have done them better. The credit belongs to the man who is actually in the arena, whose face is marred by dust and sweat and blood; who strives valiantly; who errs, who comes short again and again, because there is no effort without error and shortcoming; but who does actually strive to do the deeds; who knows great enthusiasms, the great devotions; who spends himself in a worthy cause; who at the best knows in the end the triumph of high achievement, and who at the worst, if he fails, at least fails while daring greatly, so that his place shall never be with those cold and timid souls who neither know victory nor defeat.

Theodore Roosevelt
From 'Citizenship in a Republic', Paris, 23 April, 1910

INTRODUCTION

About half a million dollars. That's how much the taxpayer has paid for me to be here writing this today. I didn't receive it as a cheque, direct debit, or cash; I received it as something far more valuable — life-saving medical treatment at Christchurch Hospital. If it wasn't for our healthcare system, I'd be in a box in the ground now. I don't underestimate the significance of this, the luck I had to be born in a country with a healthcare system like ours, the luck I had to be treated by such an incredible medical team made up of such incredible people, and my luck to be able to be here today — none of it is lost on me.

I learnt a lot in the time I spent in hospital — a lot about myself, about life, about death, and how underpaid nurses are, and about anti-nausea medication. And some of the things that I learnt have changed my life for the better by far. They have made me a better person.

I've also realised that, now I have beaten cancer, people think I have some amazing life advice to dish out, that the secrets of life are hidden somewhere in bags of chemotherapy drugs.

The truth is, I'm not qualified to give out any kind of life advice — I'm a 19-year-old kid. What I am qualified to tell you about is how lucky you are to be here right now, because that's something I understand, and also what having cancer has taught me.

1 | BC – BEFORE CANCER

Before any of this happened, I was just a very normal teenager. Okay, I was head boy — or senior monitor as it's known at my school Christchurch Boys' High School — but I still did all the things that a normal teenage boy would do. I had a bit of a reputation for being a monitor who was more focused on enjoying life than achieving straight As, even though I had ambitions. That is not to say I didn't take my responsibilities very seriously, because I did. But when I was 'off duty' I pushed my limits. Some of that came from the pressure of being head boy and the stress that came with it. I didn't do drugs or hurt others, but every weekend I embraced being young. As I said in the speech I gave at my school's end-of-year prizegiving, there is a point at which parents need to step back and give young people the space to make our own choices, to become the people we will be.

I was exploring. I still joke about how I probably gave myself cancer. On a normal weekend, I'd go out partying, sleep for four hours, eat takeaways, and do dumb things like riding in car boots — I guess it could be seen as normal teenage boy stuff. To some people, the things I used to do might seem immature for a person who had been put in a position of responsibility, but it was me learning to celebrate my life. Not doing anything too harmful — I was just having a laugh.

Some of my desire to appreciate life may have come from an awareness of death. Seven months before I was made head boy, I sat at the bedside of my nana, my mum's mum, Elaine Berry, as cancer took her. We were incredibly close. For most of my life I felt like there was no age gap between us. She was vibrant, kind, humorous and wise and, having lost a son and a husband, she talked a lot about enjoying life and appreciating the little things. In fact, one of her regular comments when she enquired about my latest adventures was: 'Good on you, Jake! None of us get out of life alive.' They are not her words originally, but she is the one who fixed that idea firmly in my head.

We nursed Nana in her home, and watching her go cut me deep. Growing up, I seemed to go to more funerals than most adults. My middle name came from my father's uncle, Ross (also my father's name), who died just before I was born. At six, a teacher I adored died. At age seven, I saw my beloved grandfather dead on the floor after a sudden heart attack. In the few years BC, I lost other relatives, family friends and, most unexpectedly, a cousin in a car accident. I ended up owning a 'funeral outfit' that hung in my closet ready to go.

I remember sitting at Nana's funeral and hearing all the funny adventures she'd had. Nana used to say kindness was her religion, but she was never too serious about it — she was brilliant fun to be around. It struck me then that I had to make life a daring adventure. Maybe that was when my focus shifted from trying to take out class prizes to making sure there was always lots of laughter, too.

I guess, at times, there has been two of me. The 'head boy' me and the daring, adventurous me, and I worked to keep the two worlds apart. Cancer made this impossible. It blurred the edges. I kept some of what I'd done from other people, probably in case they thought less of me. But facing death strips things back to the rawest they can get. So here it all is, laid out on the table. One of the things I have learnt on this journey is that when I make a speech or do an interview, different parts of what I say speak to different people. Some of what I say will be for the teenager with cancer, other parts will speak to the parent, whose child has gone into battle. Whoever you are, I hope you find something of worth.

PLANS DON'T ALWAYS WORK OUT

My final year at school was a really busy time for me, I was head boy, and after turning 18 I began working part-time in a bar. So, on a Wednesday, I'd have school from 9am until 2.30pm then I'd go home and sleep for a couple of hours. Then I'd go to work and be at the bar from 9pm until we closed. Unfortunately, closing time varied and, at its worst, it went a few hours into the next day. Then I'd go home, have a shower, sleep a couple of hours and be up at 7am, running late and racing out the door for school. Although it was only on Wednesdays, it definitely took its toll on me. My weekends were always super busy as well. Aside from socialising, I worked hard on my studies and my commitments as senior monitor as well. I took these very seriously.

I remember one occasion, in the middle of the year, when I had a bad cold. I sat shivering in front of the heater after dinner, but insisted on getting up to go to an Old Boys' meeting at school, while my mother, Janine Harrington, argued that I should be getting into bed instead. I also played football for two teams in the winter, but I broke my thumb about halfway through the season, which put me on the bench for the rest of the games. That was my first ever hospital experience. I even lied to my parents so they didn't have to worry about it, and told them I was going to a mate's place when I was really taking myself off to Accident and Emergency. Little did I know what was to come.

Despite the pace, it was the best year of my life. It was full on but it was fantastic, and I was having a hell of a lot of fun. The monitors were a great bunch of young men to be working and socialising with. Basically, I felt like I had to make the most of my final year, because after school everything was going to change. Things would become more serious.

I planned to commence a double degree in commerce and law at the University of Auckland in 2016. I'd been to Auckland on holiday a couple of times, and I decided that it was the place for me. I found the place quite intoxicating — the size of the city, the fast cars, partying at the Viaduct, a world I'd never seen up close before. I thought I wanted some of that, along with a job in the corporate world. But until then I wanted to make the most of my last year in Christchurch. And then my body hatched an incredibly elaborate plan to get me out of my end-of-year exams.

KEEP ASKING QUESTIONS

Somewhere in amongst all that busy time, I started getting pain in my wisdom teeth. The lower two had started to come through, but I had pain only on one side. My usual dentist was away so, on 16 September, I went to see a locum as I thought the teeth were impacted. The dentist took an x-ray and it showed a large mass on one side. He said he could tell from the colour of it that it wasn't a cyst and it wasn't an abscess, but he didn't know what it was.

He reckoned that sometimes nerves could go a bit funny when your wisdom teeth are pushing through, so it could have been that but, as he wasn't sure, he sent me away to have the teeth removed.

In theory, I could have had this done by a dentist but, because we had health insurance, I had to go to a surgeon to get a report for the insurance company saying that I definitely needed to have the teeth out. It was the insurance company that then insisted I have a maxillofacial surgeon — who specialises in operating on the mouth and the jaw — take my teeth out. Because there was a shortage of such surgeons in Christchurch, the appointments were very few and far between and I was initially told that I would have to wait until January just to see someone, which seemed like a very long time to be in so much pain and unable to eat. Thankfully, due to my mother's persistent and well-intentioned nagging, the appointment was brought forward to just three weeks away.

I'm guessing I'd probably had the pain for about a week to two weeks before that. Given what I know now, the cancer had probably been there for about a month. On 15 August my school's first XV had been kicked out of the Christchurch rugby championships by Shirley Boys' High School, who were one of our main rivals. I've joked since that it was losing to Shirley that gave me cancer. Well, it was either that or the huge celebratory night I had when I turned 18 the next day.

The pain in my wisdom teeth was awful. Breaking my thumb had nothing on this level of pain. All I could do was pace around to try to distract myself. I had codeine left over from when I broke my thumb, so I'd take a couple of those, but even they didn't take the edge off.

I went to the maxillofacial surgeon for my initial consultation, after which there was a whole lot of back and forth between the surgeon and my dentist. Then there were second opinions to be obtained from the hospital. Everything required an appointment, and it seemed everyone was booked up. We were on a conveyer belt and we couldn't speed up the process.

At this stage, there were no suggestions it was anything more sinister than wisdom teeth that wouldn't play ball. But, in the meantime, the pain was gradually getting worse. It spread from one side of my face and started to affect the other side as well. The skin around my jaw started going this weird purple colour. Then I lost feeling on and off around my lower lip and chin.

On 9 October, I had a coffee with Jemima, a girl I had been seeing for a few months. We weren't dating at the time but we'd been hanging out together a lot. The reason she wanted to meet me that day was to tell me she didn't want to take our relationship any further because she was so busy. It was the start of the athletics season — she's a 400m track athlete — and she also had end-of-year exams coming up. She didn't think she had time for a boyfriend as well. Plus, she was planning to move to Australia at the end of the year (she's an Australian citizen and was going back for university and her sport), so she didn't want either of us to get too attached.

I was feeling pretty flat about it, so I drove down to Timaru to see some friends. As I was driving back from Timaru, the pain kicked in again. This time, I lost the feeling in my chin and it didn't come back. It's returned now, but it's still a very altered sensation — the area just below my lip remains really tickly and sensitive.

By this stage I'd also dropped a bit of weight. At the time I thought it was just because I hadn't been able to eat solid food for a while but actually it was because my body was fighting so hard against the cancer.

When I got back from my trip to Timaru, a friend invited me to his house and it turned out Jemima was visiting a friend next door. We caught up and, although I was feeling rubbish, we stayed up until late talking and I managed to change her mind about the whole relationship thing that night. We talked about taking chances, and I went from being dumped to having a girlfriend all in the same day.

A few days later, at the end of the school holidays, I went to bed and just couldn't get up the next morning. I was absolutely broken. My whole face felt like I'd had a local anaesthetic and, to add to that, I would throw up every time I ate.

The dentist had given me some painkillers, which helped a bit, and he'd also given me some anti-inflammatories to reduce what he thought was swelling. The idea was that they'd bring the swelling down, which would release the nerves and allow the feeling in my face to come back. I was meant to be taking the anti-inflammatories with food, but I couldn't eat. I don't know if it was taking them on an empty stomach or the cancer, but I started throwing up blood. My body was slowly shutting down.

By this time, I had two dentists and two maxillofacial surgeons trying to work out what was wrong with me and what they should do about it. No one seemed to know what was going on.

Once I started throwing up blood — on my mum's carpet for maximum horror movie-style effect — we decided it was time to head to Accident and Emergency. The doctors there didn't think it was anything too serious but they did some tests, which showed that my kidney function was really altered. The doctors thought it was a result of my body being dehydrated from vomiting or digesting my own blood, when it was actually because my kidneys were full of tumours. I know now that they were the size of massive grapefruits — they're usually the size of fists — because they were so full of cancer. No follow-up was booked and I was sent home within two hours — at 4.30am.

At home I headed back to bed. School had gone back, but I didn't have the energy to get dressed, let alone get out of the house. The waiting time between appointments seemed endless. But as the next appointment available for the surgeon to remove my teeth wasn't until January, I thought I'd just have to put up with feeling terrible until then. The prospect of not being able to eat solid food for three months was pretty grim — little did I know that I could have been dead by then.

During this time, I was referred for an MRI by a hospital maxillofacial surgeon. My mum rang daily to find out when the appointment would be. She was told that she just needed to be patient. After a week of these phone calls, the hospital finally admitted that the form had been lost and I was told that the appointment would be 'triaged'. Their idea of treating something with urgency and Mum's differed a bit, because the form didn't come through until three weeks later and, thankfully, by then I was already in hospital having chemo.

The dentist then decided to take two of my wisdom teeth out himself, as he could see I was in a really bad way and he thought it might help. As he took one tooth out, I heard him say, 'That doesn't look too good!' which isn't really what you want to hear when you're lying there in the dentist's chair. He took photos of the tooth and then scrubbed chunks of tumour off the rest of my teeth (without realising what it was) and gave the extracted teeth to me to take home. They sat on my beside table while I lay in bed dying.

At that point, everyone thought I'd start feeling better because the teeth were gone, and because what I thought was an infection would clear up. Of course, neither of those things occurred. In fact, I started feeling worse. Up until that point, everything had had a rational explanation. I was throwing up blood because my stomach was stripped by the anti-inflammatories. I was losing weight because I wasn't eating solid food. I'd lost feeling in my face because there was an abscess pressing on the nerves. It all made sense. Except, of course, there was something much more sinister going on.

Things could have happened differently. They could have been better. They could have been worse. At the end of the day, I still would have had cancer. I don't believe that either one of those things will benefit from being dissected too thoroughly. It is what it is.

2 | DIAGNOSIS

Because I was still so unwell, on 22 October I had appointments with not one but two maxillofacial surgeons. I saw the hospital maxillofacial in the morning and the private one in the afternoon. I was really ill at this stage, and it felt to us like no one was taking us seriously. No one seemed to believe that the pain could be that bad, or that I was really as sick as I was. It seemed that as far as they were concerned, I had infected wisdom teeth, not enough sleep and a low pain tolerance.

Thankfully, at my afternoon appointment, the private maxillofacial surgeon said I needed to be admitted to hospital. He sent me off to A&E and told me to tell them that he'd sent me.

The A&E team did some blood tests and, as I was

waiting for the results to come through, a terrible thought came into my mind — maybe I had contracted hepatitis. I didn't know much about it, but I knew you could get it through open wounds. A few months earlier, I'd been at work at the bar and I'd cut my hand on a broken glass. For some reason I started to think that whatever was wrong with me was something I'd inflicted on myself. It certainly never occurred to me that my medical issue was one of the rarest forms of cancer in existence.

When the initial test results came through, I got sent to AMAU, the acute medical assessment unit. When a nurse came to put an IV drip into my arm, she shaved the hair off first. I remember thinking 'Jeez, I'm going to look pretty silly with one hairless arm' — little did I know how much worse it was going to get!

I was kept in overnight — the first time I'd ever stayed in hospital. Up until then, I hadn't been to the doctor in three years because I just never got sick. In fact, my GP rang my mother several times during my treatment to ask how I was going. On his first call, he admitted that he couldn't remember what I looked like as he hadn't seen me in such a long time.

Being in hospital was a really weird experience. I didn't sleep at all the first few nights I was there. The AMAU seemed like it was pretty much just for old people who were groaning and dying. That was a bit unnerving for me. At about four o'clock one morning, I heard them wheeling a woman past my cubicle and she was screaming, 'I'm dying! I'm dying!' I ended up doing the same thing about three days later, which was kind of ironic.

Up until about two or three days before I was diagnosed, I still thought I'd wake up one morning and be fine. There was no reason for me to believe otherwise. Even when I was in hospital, I'd be thinking that if I got a good night's sleep, I'd wake up the next day and feel well enough to go home. That didn't end up happening.

I didn't really think too much about what was going on. I just went along with what I was being told — there always seemed to be a rational explanation for everything. I guess it was good that I wasn't too stressed about my situation. It was probably worse for my family, who took turns sitting with me and my dad, Ross, chose to sleep by my bed most nights.

I had to get a whole heap of tests done — a CT scan, a bone marrow aspiration, a kidney biopsy, and a gum biopsy — all in close succession. Why a biopsy on my gums? Well, the tumours had grown so much they were coming out of the sockets where I'd had my teeth taken out. They were so big I couldn't close my mouth, which was probably quite handy for the doctors trying to identify what was wrong — the cancer was pretty much climbing out of my face to say hi to them. Even more gross was that I could see them in the mirror. Mum reckoned they looked like grey cauliflowers.

My tumours were doubling in size every 24–48 hours. With my type of cancer, they grow so fast you can almost see them expanding. Pretty much all of the tests I had to diagnose what was wrong with me were really horrible and even now, I'd rather not think about them.

The bone marrow aspiration was probably the worst. To get a sample to test, they put this really long needle right into the bone at the back of my hip, breaking through the outer bone to get at the liquid bone marrow inside. That hurt more than my wisdom teeth extraction and I yelled out in pain when they did it. I had inadvertently become one of those people whose yelling and groaning would have been unnerving to those new to the ward. The doctor said they'd give me medication so that I wouldn't remember having the procedure. Given that I remember her saying that, I'm guessing whatever they gave me didn't work!

A couple of weeks before, I'd been getting these really bad aching pains in my legs. It got much worse in the days I spent at home in bed. At the time, I remember thinking it felt like it was inside the bone. It turned out that it was — it was the bone marrow producing cancer cells.

Blood tests showed that my kidneys were failing more each day. On my way to get my kidney biopsy, the pain in my legs was overwhelming. It was so bad that when I opened my eyes while they were wheeling me to the operating theatre, I couldn't see anything — there was just this white light. Later Mum and I discussed whether the white light was that light some people think you walk towards when you die. I don't think it was. It's just that the pain was overriding everything, including my ability to focus my eyes. That was when I started crying out, 'Mum, I'm dying!' I was pretty much bang on. I was dying.

THE MEDICAL STUFF

ULTRASOUND
During an ultrasound, high-frequency sound waves are aimed at your internal organs. These will echo differently when they are bounced off abnormal tissues, like tumours.

MRI
MRI scans — otherwise known as magnetic resonance imaging scans — combine magnetism and radio waves to make up a picture of the inside of the body. From looking at the scans, doctors can sometimes tell whether a tumour is cancerous or not. They can also see how far a tumour has spread.

CT SCAN
CT scans are also sometimes known as CAT scans, which stands for computerised (axial) tomography scans. Basically, a CT scan is a whole lot of x-rays taken from different angles. These are all put together by a computer to give a detailed picture of the inside of your body. The cross-sections that a CT scan produces give an accurate picture of the location and size of any tumours.

BONE MARROW ASPIRATE

Otherwise known as a bone marrow aspiration, this involves sticking a needle into a large bone to remove a small sample of bone marrow. This can then be tested to check whether there is any cancer present. Bone marrow contains cells that produce both white and red blood cells and platelets, low levels of which are a strong indicator of the presence of cancer.

KIDNEY AND GUM BIOPSIES

The kidney biopsy involved a thin needle being inserted through my skin and into my kidney to remove a small piece of tissue. This tissue was then analysed to see if there were cancerous cells present.

The gum biopsy was similar, in that a piece of my gum was removed and tested to help identify the tumours that were growing in my mouth.

They knocked me out and did the kidney biopsy. Before the results came through, some of the doctors thought it was lymphoma and others thought it was a type of autoimmune disease. The first time a doctor came in and explained that I might have lymphoma, Mum said, 'What's that?' I cut in and replied, 'It's cancer.'

Before the kidney biopsy, I had to get an emergency CT scan. It took 36 hours because one of the scanners was broken. On top of that, it was Labour Weekend, so there wasn't anyone on duty who could do my biopsies. We had to wait until after the weekend. It might only have been three days, but that was enough time for the tumours to double in size. I guess all of this delayed the start of my treatment, but it didn't affect the outcome, so it's hard to be too upset about it. By then, the doctors knew something was wrong and the race was on.

I found out later that I was the talk of the hospital at the time. My type of cancer is so rare that everyone had an opinion about what it might be, and the doctors were having meetings trying to get to the bottom of it all.

Then, one afternoon, the doctor who was to become my main haematologist came into my room, sat by my bed and told me, slowly and calmly, that I had stage four Burkitt's non-Hodgkin's lymphoma, the most aggressive kind of cancer. It was presenting in my kidneys, eye sockets, nasal passage, membrane around my brain, bone marrow, spinal fluid, cheek and jaw. That was just where they'd found it at that stage — for the next few days they kept coming in and updating me as to its locations, as the team analysing my results expanded. Without treatment I was given two to three weeks to live, and no guarantee of survival if I received treatment.

YOU DON'T KNOW WHAT'S AROUND THE NEXT CORNER

When my haematologist first told me that I had a good chance of beating Burkitt's, I thought, 'What does she mean "I'll probably be able to beat it"? Of course I'll beat it. I'm not going to die from this.'

I truly believe that optimism was hugely powerful in my battle with cancer. That was my mindset right from the start. I never considered dying an option. I don't think it was even a conscious decision to adopt that attitude. My brain just didn't allow me to entertain the possibility.

It was similar to my perspective on the things that had happened in my life to date that I would have preferred to be different, like my parents' separation or the loss of loved ones. I was tempted to wrestle against it, but I know there is no point fighting what you can't change. Moving quickly into acceptance and then action mode was better for me than losing the plot.

Acceptance is not apathy or resignation, but it does make a huge difference to your headspace. It is about coming to terms with the reality of a given situation. It is important to understand that accepting something does not imply you are happy about it. You can dislike

THE MEDICAL STUFF

CANCER STAGES

Many cancer diagnoses have a stage number between one and four attached to them. One is the least serious and four is the most serious. These stages are usually thought to mean:

- Stage One: The cancer is relatively small and found only in the site where it started.
- Stage Two: The cancer is a bit bigger, but hasn't spread into the surrounding tissue.
- Stage Three: The cancer is larger and may have started to spread into surrounding tissue.
- Stage Four: The cancer has spread from where it started into other organs of the body. In the case of lymphoma, stage four means that the cancer has spread out of the lymph nodes, for example, to the bone marrow, kidneys or central nervous system.

BURKITT'S

Named after Denis Burkitt, the doctor who first identified this form of lymphoma in 1958 after seeing it in young people in Africa.

LYMPHOMA

This is a type of cancer that originates in the white blood cells within the lymphatic system. The lymphatic system is a part of the body's immune system which helps to clean the body of bacteria, viruses and other harmful toxins. The increase in abnormal white cells, lymphoma cells, causes some lymph nodes to increase in size.

NON-HODGKIN'S

All types of lymphoma are classified as non-Hodgkin's, except the ones where a specific abnormal cell (called a Reed-Sternberg cell) is present. If that cell is detected, then the lymphoma is defined as being Hodgkin's.

situations and still accept them. Finding ways to accept those things that are beyond your control to change provides freedom from having to fight against the situations you find yourself in unwittingly.

People would say to me, 'You're so brave!' I never tried to be brave, and I was no more brave than anyone else on the ward. I never tried to feel a certain way. I never tried to do things a certain way. It was what it was. I guess what I know now is that bravery is not a lack of fear, but the ability to move forward despite fear. I knew I needed to march forward. I thought of it as 'going over the top', out of the trenches to assault the enemy in battle. Of course, first I would have to cross 'no man's land'.

One thing I did have on my side was the grit of a teenager. Part of being a teenager is thinking that you're ten foot tall and bulletproof — I was no different. When I was told that I had cancer I didn't feel or think much, I was a bit surprised, of course, but nothing else — not angry, not scared, not upset or despondent. I was just aware that I now had a fight on my hands, and I needed to get on with it. There was nothing I could do about it now but begin the chemo.

After the doctor told Mum, Dad, Uncle Steve, Auntie Katrina and me that I had cancer, she then asked the others to step outside with her, so she could speak to them about what was happening. She told them that without treatment, I would live for only about two to three weeks. She also told them that given my kidneys were failing, and I was already so close to death, the treatment would be gruelling and that it might even kill me if I elected to have it.

When they came back in, Mum rushed over and hugged me and started to cry. I told her that if she had to cry then she would have to leave. It was time for me to step up and, given the urgency, I had no time to wallow. I had already put my game face on.

I said to Uncle Steve, 'Pick a star sign beginning with C!'. He said, 'Capricorn?' I said, 'No, the doctor says I've got the other one.' It took him a moment to work out what I was talking about, and he just cracked up laughing. My family has a history of laughing our way through tough times — and I was determined that wasn't going to change now. A positive attitude was our best chance through, and I knew Steve wouldn't let me down in humour or hard times. He was one of the many I'd need next to me as I went into this.

THERE'S NO EASY WAY TO TELL SOMEONE YOU HAVE CANCER

When I got told I had cancer, I didn't actually feel anything. I know that sounds a bit weird. Most people would expect to feel angry, or scared, or afraid, or all of the above. I felt none of them. I felt nothing at all. There was a bit of relief in knowing what was actually wrong with me, but I very quickly put all of my focus into getting through the treatment. I suppose it would have been different if I was diagnosed and had to go home and digest the prognosis. But because I was already in hospital and my treatment had to start straight away, there was no time for contemplation. I was very focused on the future and what I needed to do. The part that was a real challenge was having to tell other people.

Jemima and I had only been dating for 10 days when I was diagnosed. She was at St Margaret's College and we'd met through some mates. By the time she arrived to see me at the hospital, I'd only seen her once since we'd officially started dating because I'd been so sick. The second time she had come to see me in hospital — so our third time together since being a couple, I guess — I had to tell her I had cancer.

I said, 'The doctors know what's wrong, but I'm not sure I should tell you.' Given she had had reservations about our relationship because of her other commitments, a cancer diagnosis didn't seem like it would help the situation.

She looked at me as if to say, 'You've got to be kidding me!' But she actually said, 'I think you should probably tell me.' I had no choice but to come out with it. 'Umm, okay, yeah, I've got cancer. It's called Burkitt's non-Hodgkin's lymphoma.'

I felt like it was horribly unfair on her. I told her, 'Run for the hills. It's going to get really messy and really bad really fast. You need to get out of here because this isn't what you signed up for. This isn't what you deserve. I'm not going to blame you if you do. No one is going to blame you for doing it. For your own sake, run for the hills.'

She wasn't having a bar of it. 'No, we're going to get through this together.'

I couldn't believe it. I was pretty impressed, because that's not what you do when you've been with someone for 10 days and they tell you that they might die. You don't stick around to see how it will end; you get the hell out as fast as you can. That was moral strength right there. The courage of someone who had the option to take the easy road but chose to stand strong in the face of adversity. It was also the first time I understood that this was not just my battle but that of those around me. Their lives had all been altered in a heartbeat, too.

Once I'd told Jemima, I lay awake for ages. At 2am, I called another one of my mates and told him I had cancer. It was a school night so, obviously, I'd woken him up and he wasn't thinking all that clearly, and with the pain meds I was on, I wasn't making too much sense either. He ended up with the impression that it was terminal cancer — it was two days later, when they announced it at school, that he found out that I wasn't, in fact, dying and that the prognosis was pretty good. I felt a bit stink about that.

I wasn't sure how to tell the rest of my mates. I mean, it's not something you ever imagine yourself having to do, is it? In typical teenage fashion, I left it until the very last minute. I knew that the school was about to announce at assembly that I had cancer, so I had 20 minutes to let a whole lot of them know before everyone else found out too. What to do? Well, I just put it in a group text. It went something like this:

Hey guys, what are we doing this weekend?

I hear there's a party out at Lincoln.

What's for lunch?

Hey guys, docs say I've got cancer.

Probably not the most emotionally intelligent thing I could have done, but I kind of hoped that everyone would just keep scrolling and no one would pick up on it. I felt weirdly guilty about telling them, because I didn't want to ruin their day. But, of course, they did notice it — no one's going to ignore that kind of announcement.

Thankfully, after the initial shock, the jokes starting coming. Most of them seemed to revolve around my eyebrows and hair falling out.

I didn't really want anyone to know that I was sick. One of our family friends texted me to say they were sorry to hear about the diagnosis. It was a really lovely message, but as I read it my stomach dropped. This was the first time in my diagnosis I felt angry. I didn't want anything to change just because I had cancer. If I'd had it my way, I'd have gone to hospital, had my three months of treatment and not told anybody. I don't know why. I guess I didn't want anyone to pity me or change the way they were towards me.

That said, I was fine with everyone at school being told I was sick. An email was read out in class so everyone found out at the same time. I don't know why my schoolmates knowing didn't worry me, but other people finding out did.

3 | STARTING TREATMENT

TAKE NOTHING FOR GRANTED

So, where to from there? You're 18, you're told that you could die within weeks; that everything you have been promised since you were a child — the house, the family, the nice job — might never arrive. You're told the next months — the laughs, the parties, the classes, the lunches with mates — will never happen because you'll be in a hospital bed. You're told that everything you assumed would always be available to you, things upon which your foundation is built — the outings with family, the embrace of your girlfriend, the sunrise on your face — might not be yours to feel any longer. You're told that your time is up — if not the time that is your life, then certainly the time when you had it easy. You know you've got an advantage — you're young and fit — but then again, you don't want to take anything for granted.

After the diagnosis, I went straight to the BMTU — the bone marrow transplant unit — which is one of the treatment areas for those with blood cancers, including leukaemia and lymphoma, and where I was about a third of the average age of every other patient.

I remembered having been to hospital to visit my nana with Dad when I was about eight. We walked past the bone marrow transplant unit and — being a typical inquisitive kid — I asked Dad why people had to have bone marrow transplants. He said, 'I think it's something to do with cancer.' He was right.

Arriving at the BMTU was confronting. I could see other people all around me who were battling cancer. They were thin and bald, shuffling along the corridor, looking frail and gaunt. I found the sight pretty shocking until I realised that was pretty much what I looked like, except — for now — I still had my hair.

The BMTU is the most isolated part of the hospital. You have to go through four different doors and an airlock to get in there. Then you have to sanitise your hands a couple of times before you go into a room. The air system is HEPA filtered, which removes 99.97 per cent of particles. All this is done because pretty much everyone in the unit has crashed immune systems, either as a result of their illness or as a result of their treatment. This meant that I wasn't allowed many visitors, which suited me fine. I didn't want people to see me so sick and didn't feel up to having many people around me.

Given the ward I was in, I asked the doctors if I'd have to have a bone marrow transplant. They told me that it was an option further down the line if I needed it. That seemed fair enough. The first plan of attack was a specially devised set of six rounds of chemotherapy treatments designed for my condition.

There was a risk that the chemo wouldn't work, so the doctors were always looking for a plan B, just in case. It was a real race for them, as they'd estimated that, at the cancer's current rate of growth, without treatment it would be about 14 days before I died. That wasn't long for them to get the prescribed treatment right for what was a rare disease.

One thing I did have to do right away was store sperm. It was quite a weird thing to have to think about at such a young age, but there was the possibility that the chemo would make me infertile so putting a few on ice would give me options down the track. It probably would have been better if the suggestion hadn't been floated in front of my school principal, who was visiting me at the time, but I guess it made for a great work story for Mr Hill!

The day after I moved to the BMTU, I was taken to the fertility clinic. Okay, let's get it out of the way. Given how sick I was, it wasn't done how you probably think. It involves needles — four of them to be exact — being put in places that you really don't want needles. I don't remember much about it as I was really zonked out. I'd been bedridden for weeks, I was dosed up on morphine, I'd just found out I had stage four cancer and there was a possibility I could die, yet there I was at the fertility clinic. Sitting in the waiting room was almost weirder than getting the needles poked in me. I'm pretty sure there weren't too many 18-year-old guys visiting that day.

Once they'd got the sperm stowed away, I went back to the BMTU where a PICC line was put in ready to start chemo the next day. PICC stands for peripherally inserted central catheter, and it's basically a tube that is put into a vein in your arm and then guided through your body using a wire until it reaches your heart — my first one was 36 centimetres long. The line is then used to hook you up to machinery that administers medicine, like chemotherapy drugs and antibiotics, and sometimes nutrition over a long period of time.

CHEMO IS NOTHING LIKE WHAT YOU SEE ON TV

What I knew about chemo was what I'd seen on TV. I knew I'd probably get sick, but I had no idea how sudden the changes would be or how long it would take for my hair to fall out. I didn't know anything.

At this point, I still felt incredibly ill. I was being poked and prodded and I was still dying. I did not pray to live, instead I asked that if cancer was to be the thing that killed me, that I faced it with strength. If it was going to kill me, it would do so on my terms, and I would not die a coward — not wanting to let fear dictate my death any more than it had my life. But I was still determined to beat it. There was not a chance in hell that I was prepared to die when I hadn't even finished school yet.

At the start of the treatment process, I had quite a weird idea of what was going to happen. I remember thinking, 'Thank goodness it happened over Christmas so I can get it done and I can still go to uni next year. I'll miss a bit of school, but I'll do my three months of treatment and then life will go back to normal.' Little did I know it didn't quite work like that.

The actual chemo was pretty straightforward. There was a bag marked 'toxic' hooked up to a machine, which was hooked up to the line in my arm. The stuff in the bag dripped into my arm for however long it took to be finished, and I'd think of it as containing all the moments of my future. Some of the chemo doses took five minutes to be administered, some lasted for 24 hours, but most of them took about 45 minutes. I might have one or two or even three a day, depending on where I was in the cycle.

The prescribed therapy for my type of lymphoma was alternating courses of two different types of chemotherapy regimens — R-CODOX-M and R-IVAC.

The first time I had the rituximab I had a really bad reaction to it. I was lying there and suddenly felt quite cold. I pulled the blankets up, but just got colder and colder and couldn't stop shaking. I felt like I was

THE MEDICAL STUFF

The two different types of chemotherapy I was given were R-CODOX-M and R-IVAC.

R-CODOX-M is made up of:
- rituximab
- cyclophosphamide
- vincristine (which is also known as Oncovin)
- doxorubicin
- methotrexate

R-IVAC is made up of:
- rituximab
- etoposide
- ifosfamide
- cytarabine

The cyclophosphamide was given daily over five days, and the methotrexate took 24 hours for a single dose. The cytarabine and methotrexate were injected into my veins as well as being given through intrathecal injections. The ifosfamide and etoposide were both given daily over five days. Rituximab is an antibody treatment which specifically targets the lymphoma cells and is given over a few hours.

having a seizure. The nurse pressed the emergency button it was so bad. Suddenly, there were three doctors and about six nurses standing around me, putting me on oxygen and pumping me full of stuff to stop the reaction. I was wrapped up with all these blankets on top of me, but in order to access my PICC line they had to pull back the covers a few centimetres. I couldn't handle the cold that came with having even a small amount of my skin exposed to the air. Eventually, I was given a sedative and I woke up a bit later wondering what the hell had happened.

Once I got used to it, the chemo didn't make me violently ill or anything. It just looked like a bag of water that was being dripped into my arm, and that's how I thought of it. I never quite knew how I'd react to each dosage. Later in the day, I might feel shit or I might not, I might feel like eating or I might not; it was all quite unpredictable. Watching a bag of stuff labelled 'toxic' dripping into my body was quite a weird experience. After years of being taught to stay away from chemicals, not breathe in car fumes or fly spray, to wash my fruit before I eat it — all to, ironically, avoid getting cancer — having a bag of something toxic dripping into me was surreal.

I think I handled the chemo pretty well because I'd felt so bad before I started having it. I was so close to dying that a bit of chemo didn't really make too much difference to the general level of shittiness that I felt. I reckon that if a 'healthy' person had chemo it would feel like the worst thing in the world, but for me it was an improvement. I had been so close to total systemic shutdown that having something in me that was fighting to keep me alive felt good.

ALWAYS ASK ABOUT ANAESTHETICS

One thing that didn't feel good was the lumbar punctures. Called intrathecal injections, these procedures were designed to inject chemotherapy drugs directly into the fluid that surrounded my brain and my spinal cord. They were a regular part of my chemo treatment, and it's fair to say they were the most traumatic time for me. Even though I was given some relaxants, they didn't seem to work. I was also given laughing gas, and that didn't work either.

Basically, an intrathecal involves having a needle stuck between your vertebra right through the membrane, into the fluid which surrounds the spinal cord. If you think it sounds bad, I can assure you it's even worse. It's hard to describe the popping sensation I felt when that long needle broke through, and the incredible shooting pains I had in my legs when it hit nerves within the column, or the pressure I felt in my back when the needle hit bone. All while the room was blinding bright white, and I couldn't make sense of anything anyone was saying because of the amount of laughing gas I'd sucked down.

Ironically, about a month before I was first diagnosed, some guys and I had been talking about lumbar punctures in class. Someone had been given one when the doctors thought he might have meningococcal meningitis. After a quick chat about the process, I said that I could never have a lumbar puncture because even the thought of the process made me squeamish. Two months later I was having one every couple of days.

I remember during one of these intrathecal procedures, the doctor couldn't get the needle into my spinal column. After that, my anxiety around lumbar punctures increased tenfold. I would be given increasing doses of drugs before them, to try to relax me, but they didn't help. I just had to remind myself that this was chemo I needed to save my life, and the clock was ticking. At one stage, it got to the point that whenever the doctor who administered my lumbar puncture walked past my room, my heart rate would go through the roof and my stomach would start churning.

One of Mum's friends, who works in medicine, seemed surprised that I wasn't being given a general anaesthetic to knock me out before the lumbar punctures, since I was still pretty young. We asked the doctors about this, and they seemed to have a light-bulb moment, as they realised I was only a couple of months over the cut-off for being treated as a child. From then on, they decided to do my lumbar punctures in the children's ward under general anaesthetic, for which I am immensely grateful.

I'm quite proud that, as a result of my experience, Christchurch Hospital collaborates much more closely with the children's oncology team to offer general anaesthetic to patients under the age of 25. If something good has come from my worst experiences, then they have been of some worth.

The cancer had been growing so fast that the chemo was working really fast as well. After the first week, some of the feeling came back in my jaw and my chin, and that felt amazing. I was pretty relieved that the treatment was working, because if it hadn't, the doctors would have had a week left to try to work out what else they could do for me.

The first couple of weeks were really critical because, not only were my kidneys full of cancer, they were also working overtime to flush out the chemo and the toxins from the cancer. There's a condition called nephrotoxicity, where the kidneys can be damaged by this process. The possibility of my kidneys failing was pretty high, so I'd been warned that I might end up on dialysis. I found out later that, behind the scenes, my family were discussing who would donate me a kidney, not if, but when, I needed it. Thankfully, my kidneys pulled through. That was very kind of them, given they'd had a bit of a hammering from the usual teenage excesses over the previous few months.

On the fourth day of my chemotherapy, Mum decided to start sending me a daily email. It was the first of many messages that she continued to send until the 100th day of my remission. These emails are an incredible record of everything that was going on, both inside and outside the hospital while I was sick. They also make up for the fact that there are long periods during my chemotherapy that I don't remember well, on account of being so sick and sedated, so I'll include a few to fill some of the gaps in my own memory.

Day 4 of chemotherapy
Dear Jake

What I know is you are the tip of the arrow. The piece that can slice bits to shreds (these are Steve's words . . . not something from Google). Know we are behind you, backing you, and our love and support is going nowhere.

You must [grumpy voice] stop thinking about what the rest of us want (I acknowledge how accommodating and thoughtful you are as I say this), because you are the leader of this cure and we must be nothing but your obedient soldiers.

Please know our (exaggerated) actions are not about tippy-toeing around you because we are nervous. We are not. We know you are a survivor. It is about us waiting to be directed into battle.

You may have seen this in your monitors at some point. Only you can tell us (and the medical staff) what is needed and I can assure you that you have an army of people waiting for your instructions. But know if you choose not to instruct, or don't have the energy to instruct just now, we will still be loyal servants surrounding you (but maybe just walking around in circles annoying the hell out of you and asking too many questions). Our love is such.

I'm signing off now because these emails cannot become lectures. Please forgive the dumb things I have written. I write with nothing but utter and complete love for you in my heart.

With more love for you than you will ever know (until you have your own kids and nag them about how you had to have needles in your balls so they could exist), your Mum xxx

Things I am grateful for today (there will only be five a day):
1. The umpteen messages I received asking after you.
2. The doctor who raved about how well you are responding to chemo.
3. The laughter you, Uncle Steve, Auntie Katrina, Leanne, Ross and I shared in your hospital room.
4. The doctor saying the first round is the hardest and that then the chemo dose is lessened and is easier.
5. The idea from Nana to write to you.

4 | I WROTE A SPEECH

YOU'LL ONLY REGRET THE THINGS YOU DIDN'T DO

My school prizegiving, on 4 November, coincided with my fifth day of chemotherapy. I'd been in hospital for two weeks by this stage, and, as much as I wanted to, I had no idea whether I'd be able to make the traditional head boy's speech.

I was so honoured to have been appointed head boy at Boys' High. Some have suggested it was my humility, or maybe it was a fear of falling short, but I wondered if I was up to the job of being head boy — I was certainly as surprised as everyone else was when the announcement was made at the beginning of the year. It was really daunting and I hoped I could maintain the excellent example of the many great leaders before me. It was such a huge honour that I felt I owed it to the school to deliver my speech that night.

Even when I was bedridden in the weeks before I'd been diagnosed, I felt as if this was something I had to do. I so badly wanted to be all right for it.

Leading up to it, I would wonder every now and then whether I'd be well enough, but I didn't think about it a lot as I was so focused on getting better.

In the early afternoon on the day I was due to deliver the speech, Mum brought my blazer and my school uniform in to the hospital. Dad brought in a razor as well, as I hadn't shaved in three weeks by that stage. Mum told me it would be fine not to shave, but I wasn't having it. I wanted to be a presentable head boy — I had to represent the school well.

Thankfully, I'd written most of my speech before I got really sick, but I altered it slightly after I was diagnosed. It was weird how much of it was so much more relevant after I was told I had cancer. It's crazy that I was already thinking about some of life's bigger questions, even before I found out I had cancer. The one thing that is quite funny looking back is the last paragraph — 'I don't know where it goes from here for any of us — for you, for anyone, and as sure as hell not for me. But I wish you the very best in your journey, and thank you for all being part of mine. Wherever we go and whatever we do, may we always be friends when we meet again.' I was planning for the first sentence to say, 'I don't know where it goes from here for you, for me, for anyone.' I changed it to, 'and as sure as hell not for me' when I was lying in my hospital bed. Then, when I delivered it, I accidently changed it back again.

It got to about six o'clock, and it had been on and off all day whether I'd go or not. It was the day of my first lumbar puncture, so I had a really bad headache and I was feeling really shit. I was at a stage where I was simultaneously dying from cancer, having chemo, and my body was struggling to eliminate all the toxins through my failing kidneys. It was a rough day.

As time ticked on, I had to make the decision whether I'd make it. My parents had a wheelchair ready to wheel me out of the hospital to the car. I decided to get up and have a shave to see whether I felt up to going. I got about halfway through shaving and started throwing up from the sheer exhaustion. It was quite a bit like a really bad hangover — one of those ones where your body just won't let you do anything and nothing can make you feel better, where everything feels like it's blurry at the edges. But even if I multiplied the worst hangover I'd ever had in my life times 10, that wouldn't come near how awful I felt that night.

Mum hates anything to do with vomiting, so I'd say, 'Mum, you need to go out of the room. Now!' so that she didn't have to deal with my throwing up. She got used to it after a while, but it must have been pretty hard for her, especially as her mother — my nana — had died of pancreatic cancer, which meant she pretty much vomited herself to death.

I sat back down on the edge of the bed and kept throwing up into a sick bucket. One of the nurses, Georgia, came in. She was kind-hearted, funny and gentle, and we became so close that I used to joke about her being my big sister. She asked me if I was going to go. When I told her I didn't think I could, she said, 'That's fine. But I just don't want you to regret it if you don't.' She reassured me that there was no medical reason why I couldn't go — I hadn't been having chemo for long enough for my immune system to be at risk.

That gave me a bit more motivation to try, so I carried on shaving. Once that was done, I decided to see if I could manage getting my uniform on. That turned out to create a little hiccup of its own — the uniform was designed to fit me when I was 15 kilograms heavier. My belt didn't have a notch tight enough to do it up. My blazer hung off me like a cape. My pants had been tapered before and now they were really baggy. Even my shoes were too big for me. So much for making a good impression as head boy. Not to mention the fact that I hadn't washed my hair for a few days because I was too scared that it would fall out. When I look at it in the video of the speech now, I'm horrified!

Throughout the process of putting my uniform on, I stopped to throw up a few times. I even threw up my anti-nausea tablets. Once I was dressed, I sat down, exhausted, and said, 'I can't do it. I just can't do it.'

Georgia came back in and asked me again if I was

going to go. I told her I just couldn't. She said the same thing, 'It's fine if you don't go, just so long as you don't regret missing it.'

I started crying. I really wanted to go, but I just didn't know how I could make my body do it. Georgia's words of support spurred me on again. I said, 'Fuck it. I'm going to do it.' I pushed myself to the edge of the bed and sat for a minute, thinking, 'This feels like I'm in a movie. One that's pretty far-fetched, but a movie nonetheless.'

I got up and — with Mum and Georgia by my side — walked out of the hospital room, and through the airlock. I asked Georgia if she thought it would be okay if I gave her a hug. She laughed and hugged me. We both cried a bit and she told me that I'd be great. With that, Mum wheeled me out to the front of the hospital where Dad was waiting in the car.

On the way down in the lift I started violently throwing up again. Poor Mum said the sound of it was just horrific as it echoed around the lift — luckily, I wasn't bringing much up as there wasn't anything left. Well, nothing much except the dose of morphine I'd just taken for the pain. I looked at it sitting there in the bucket and wondered whether I should fish the pills out and swallow them again — that's how much I needed those painkillers. I knew I wouldn't be able to have another dose until the prescribed time, so I was going to be in pain until then.

Mum looked at me and said, 'That's it. I'm taking you back. You can't do this to yourself.' I knew she didn't want me to miss the prizegiving but she felt like she had to. But I refused to turn around. I was going to do my best to be there.

Once I was in the car, Dad and I just sat there in silence, broken only by the sound of me dry-retching every now and then. I plugged my headphones into my phone to listen to some music to try to pump myself up. The whole trip took about 15 to 20 minutes, but it passed in a complete blur.

The assembly was held in the theatre at Burnside High School, because the hall at Christchurch Boys' had been so badly damaged in the 2011 earthquakes that it had been condemned. As we arrived at Burnside High, Uncle Steve and Auntie Katrina waved us around to the carpark that had been saved for us. The whole rest of my family were there waiting for me. I later heard that Mum's texts to Steve and Katrina had gone something like this: 'It's on — see you there.' 'He can't do it.' 'He's going to try and make it.' 'He's too sick.' 'We're getting in the car!' As a result, they'd got halfway to the school before turning around and going home, where they got in and out of their car a few times before finally heading to the hall.

I got out of the car and into the wheelchair. It was quite a warm night, but I was freezing. I was shaking violently and just couldn't get warm. Someone put a coat over me but it made very little difference. I still had to have the bucket by my side because I was throwing up reasonably regularly. As I made it to the hall, I still had no idea whether I'd be able to deliver the speech or not.

A SICK BUCKET ON STAGE IS NOT A GOOD LOOK

I got wheeled through to the green room backstage. The family all went out to take their seats in the hall, leaving just me and Dad out the back. He rolled me out into the wings of the stage and while we were waiting, I hesitated. The speech was off again. I truly felt I couldn't get through it, and I said to Dad that although I wanted to be wheeled onto the stage, I wanted Nic Hill, the headmaster, to read the speech.

By chance, just as I said that, there was a big round of applause and Dad didn't hear me. He looked at me and said 'You'll be great', and began to wheel me onto the stage.

Mum had insisted that I take my sick bucket out there with me, but that was not going to happen. I gave it to Dad to look after. The other thing I left behind was my copy of my speech!

As I got out onto the stage, I turned to Mr Hill and said, 'Have you got a copy of my speech?!' He thrust his hand into his pocket and pulled out a folded piece of paper. Thank goodness. He'd been sent a copy just in case I hadn't been able to make it.

The lights shining onto the stage were so bright that I couldn't see anyone or anything. There were just vague silhouettes beyond the lights. The audience — which was made up of school-leavers, prize-winners and their families — all began to clap, and before long they were all on their feet. The teaching staff, who were sitting on the stage behind me, also rose to their feet. It felt a bit weird to be given a standing ovation when I hadn't even said anything. It was huge to receive this incredible mark of respect.

I was on the stage for about 20 minutes, but I don't remember much of it. I just kind of went on autopilot and tried not to think about anything. My main goal was not to cry. When I'd rehearsed the speech during the previous few nights, I'd always cried. There I was, lying in my hospital bed at one in the morning, reading a speech about starting a new life — and crying.

The chemo affects your blood vessels and how they dilate. As a result of this, my ears had popped and I couldn't pop them back. It felt and sounded like I had water in my ears all the time. The whole time I was giving my speech, I couldn't actually hear myself properly. The noise I could hear coming out of my mouth was really muffled. I felt like I was mumbling through a pillow, so I had no idea whether anyone could hear me properly or not.

When I got to the end, I just felt really relieved. I'd done it without throwing up. I'd done it without crying. *I'd done it.*

As I finished speaking, there was a huge impromptu haka by the other boys in my honour. That's the thing that makes me emotional when I watch it now. My cousin led it, so that made it even more special. Following that was the school song, 'Altiora Peto', which I mumbled along to as best I could.

Then it was all over and I looked at Dad and said, 'You need to get me out of here because I'm going to throw up, pass out or both.' He quickly wheeled me back into the wings, where I was reunited with my bucket. And not a minute too soon, as I started throwing up really badly. I'd held everything together for as long as I could, and now it was all falling apart again.

As I was being wheeled back out, one of my teachers came and held the door open for us. The look on his face was awful. I read it as him wondering if he'd ever see me again. The feeling was mutual — I had no idea whether I'd ever see him again either.

Everyone was waiting for me — Mum, my stepdad Matt, my little brother Harry, and that side of the family, along with my dad, my stepmum Ann-Maree, my little sister Scarlett, my grandparents Barry and Denise and all that side of the family. The whole night was so surreal. I tried to focus on the other people who were there, but I just couldn't. I knew I had to get back to hospital.

I got back into the car and lay down. I was so drained I couldn't even sit up. While Dad was putting the wheelchair into the car, I could hear family and other people sobbing outside as I lay flat on the back seat.

I'd watched my nana die of cancer just a year before, but it was nothing like how I was dying of cancer. Other ways I've seen people die have been quite peaceful. There was no peace in what I was going through. It was a brutal fight, and it was going to be one that continued until either I got better or I died. I knew that I was dying, and dying felt like a battle I'd never known.

It was a quiet drive back to hospital, broken only by the

sound of me throwing up. When we got back to my room, I didn't have the energy to get out of the wheelchair. Dad had to pick me up and put me on my bed. I just lay there on my stomach, fully dressed in my school uniform. Dad pulled my blazer and shirt off me, and took off my shoes. I was so exhausted I couldn't even move to help him.

Ironically, I was so tired that I couldn't get to sleep. I'd heard people talk about that before, but it had never happened to me. My body was shutting down in every other way but the one I wanted. I was broken down and in pain from missing that earlier morphine dose. The nurses couldn't give me any more morphine because they didn't know how much I'd digested before I threw it up. It took until midnight for anything on the anti-nausea smorgasbord to kick in and, because I couldn't hold anything down, I was given it through my PICC line. When my family asked if I wanted to see pictures and videos of me on stage, I couldn't stomach that either. I told them to put it away. I was hunkering down to fight the battle only I could.

MY SPEECH

I wrote a speech and then, a week before I was due to deliver it, they said, 'You've got cancer.' They said, 'If you don't get any treatment, you'll be dead in three weeks.' And they told me that I wouldn't be able to come and deliver this speech here tonight.

But, luckily, that speech isn't about what is to come — it's about what an amazing year it has been. You didn't really expect me to write a whole new one from my hospital bed, did you? It started like this:

'If I have seen further, it is by standing on the shoulders of giants.'

Bernard of Chartres compared us to dwarfs perched on the shoulders of giants. He pointed out that we see more and further than our predecessors, not because we have keener vision, nor greater height, but because we are lifted up and borne aloft on their gigantic stature and knowledge. Thank you, Christchurch Boys' High School for the height you offer.

Tēnā koutou katoa. Good evening, everyone, I am Jakob Ross Bailey — senior monitor of 2015.

To all the fine young men who have gone before me, and to the fine young men sitting before me, thank you for supporting me as your senior monitor this year. Yes, at times I have wondered whether I deserved this job. At times I have doubted I could get it done to the standard I thought it should be done to. But, despite my fears, I have never stopped striving to be a leader who would not let you down. And, consequently, I am grateful for what you have given to me in return. I want to share with you all some words that I hold particularly close to heart, words that meant a lot more to me this year than they ever could have before.

'It is not the critic who counts; not the man who points out how the strong man stumbles, or where the doer of deeds could have done them better. The credit belongs to the man who is actually in the arena, whose face is marred by dust and sweat and blood, who strives valiantly; who errs and comes short again and again; because there is not effort without error and shortcomings; but who does actually strive to do the deed; who knows the great enthusiasm, the great devotion, who spends himself in a worthy cause, who at the best knows in the end the triumph of high achievement and who at the worst, if he fails, at least he fails while daring greatly. So that his place shall never be with those cold and timid souls who know neither victory nor defeat.'

This job would not have been possible alone, and consequently I must thank a massive team. Firstly, to my deputies, Sam and Jesse. You have been solid and inspirational, strong where I was weak, and an amazing source of support. I always felt you had my back, and that made every day so much better. To the monitors of 2015, I owe all of you so much. I treasure the connection I have had with each and every one of you. Thank you for accepting me into a group which I could have so easily not been accepted into, for giving me a chance, for the brotherhood that we have had. Maybe the best thing that this role has given me is a connection with you all I wouldn't have had otherwise, and it means more to me than you will ever know. As I said on Monitors' Camp, you are all exceptional people of outstanding calibre, each and every one of you will go far, and I have learnt things from all of you.

I must acknowledge the sturdy leadership and support I have received from Mr Hill and the solid guidance received from Mr Fraser, Mr Williams and Mr Dunnett through this year. It has been at the core of how I have conducted myself this year, and at times I would have been very lost without your guidance. You have all taught me much, and I will carry it through life with me. Thank you for the opportunity you gave me, I hope I have done you proud.

I want to sincerely thank and acknowledge the support I have received from the Old Boys. In particular I thank you, Terry Donaldson and Jim Blair, for being men of fine character who encouraged me to walk beside you, and I have been honoured to do so. The Old Boys helped me to grasp what 130 years of history means in action. What it means to value tradition, to appreciate our rich history and to comprehend the mark the Old Boys have made on the worlds of the military, the arts and culture, commerce, law, community service and sport. I have been privileged to be supported by these wise men who spoke softly about their accomplishments, and gently of how much we have to learn and to offer — and about the responsibility that comes with that privilege. And these are the words I wrote before they sat beside my hospital bed. Thank you.

Sadly, it has been both a short and long few years, but here we are now, ready to move on, men. We've worked hard to get to this point, but haven't done it by ourselves. We have become the type of men we are, not overnight, but as a result of our decisions, the choices we make, and those who surround and support us. And it is those people we need to thank.

To our teachers, thank you for sharing your talent and knowledge, and the occasional movie. What you did for us often went beyond the call of duty. You took the time to explain assignments, repeatedly, because we weren't paying attention. You allowed us to come to you for extra help when you could have chosen not to. You put in effort to make lessons more interesting so we wouldn't just tune out. You demanded excellence from us whether or not we wanted to give it. And even to a bunch of teenage boys, it didn't go unnoticed.

To our parents, thank you for supporting us in more ways than it's easy to reconcile. Not just this year past, but for the last 13 years of school. Every day you dragged us out of bed, made sure we were semi-fed and clothed for school, then herded us out the door. You helped us with homework, paid our class fees. You came to our various events, attended our sports matches and worked with the school as required. You commiserated over our daily dramas and were there for us, but you also gave us enough space to become the men we are today.

To those sport coaches who provided us with strong counsel and guidance, thank you for making school about more than just classwork. Through our sports, we've learned how to power on through adversity and give it our best effort, win or lose. We learned the importance of discipline and good sportsmanship, and how to work closely with others to achieve a common goal — and had a lot of fun doing it.

As you heard earlier, my middle name is Ross. I was given it not long before I was born because my 'great' uncle, Ross, drowned in Sri Lanka. Mr Ross Bailey was a Christchurch-based kidney transplant surgeon working for the Asian Commission for the Global Advancement of Nephrology. He was known for making a serious difference to an extraordinary number of people's lives back when organ transplants were an amazing feat, and, all humility aside, was the best in the world at it — a true pioneer, the first person to perform a kidney transplant in New Zealand. He was also an Old Boy of Christchurch Boys' High. He came from a working-class background, the only one of his siblings to go to university, and he went on to save numerous lives because, well, he could. Because he sought higher things. His funeral saw the Cathedral in the Square bursting at the seams with people he had helped. He had done so much in his short years giving life to the dying. He dared to make a difference. A graduate of CBHS, from a working-class background, putting 'Altiora Peto' into action. Now, we can't all save lives by transplanting organs. But we can make a difference in our own way.

Christchurch Boys' High supports academic, cultural and sporting success, and as a school we are exceptional in each and every one of those fields. But we can't all be the best scholar achieving straight excellences or the best sportsman in the first XV, believe me. While we can't be the best at everything, or even, at times, even anything, what we can choose is to have moral strength. Moral strength is another of the Boys' High values. I wrote about this before I knew I had cancer. Now I have a whole new spin on it.

Moral strength is about making a conscious decision to be a person who doesn't give up, when it would be easy to. To be lesser because the journey is less arduous. Jim Rohn said, 'Let others lead small lives, but not you. Let others argue over small things, but not you. Let others cry over small hurts, but not you. Let others leave their future in someone else's hands, but not you.'

Of course, doing this will mean at some point we may have to face our fear of falling short. Fear of looking like a fool. Fear of not being enough. Being senior monitor meant facing these fears, most often daily.

Here's the thing — none of us get out of life alive, so be gallant, be great, be gracious, and be grateful for the opportunities you have. The opportunity to learn from the men who have walked before you and those who walk beside you. CBHS, I have been absent for three weeks — could you please stop sending my mother texts asking if she knows where I am every morning? That aside, I have missed you all. For the last five years I have been proud to be a student who attended Christchurch Boys' High School. And from today onwards, for the rest of my life, I will be a proud Old Boy, giving back to those before me, as they have given to me.

My challenge to each of you, and to myself, is to continue to grow, to develop for the better. The future is truly in our hands. Forget about having long-term dreams. Let's be passionately dedicated to the pursuit of short-term goals. Micro-ambitious. Work with pride on what is in front of us. We don't know where we might end up. Or when it might end up.

Some of us will not cross paths again. Some of us will likely appear on TV. Others in print. Some of us will also probably end up in prison. I have thoroughly enjoyed growing up with you all. It has been an honour and a delight to share these years with you. I know that as I look out at all of you, I will measure my time here in the friendships I've enjoyed in these last years. Some were pretty casual and others were much closer, but I'll remember each one fondly, as I'm sure you all will, too. And when many of our high school memories begin to fade, that's ultimately how we may measure the time we spent here, not in the classes, or the lunchtimes, or the exam results or years, but in the friendships that we made and the times we shared together.

And so here we stand. Our rule is over and it's up to the next class to step into our shoes and take over. I hope that those of you who follow will carry on a proud legacy. May the lads that follow benefit from the school's work to replicate the hall and the community spirit that undeniably comes from sitting together, as one, strength and character of this mighty institution combined.

I don't know where it goes from here for any of us — for you, for anyone, and as sure as hell not for me. But I wish you the very best in your journey, and thank you for all being part of mine. Wherever we go and whatever we do, may we always be friends when we meet again. Altiora Peto, lads.

5 | GOING VIRAL

DON'T BELIEVE EVERYTHING YOU READ

The following day, my family received a bunch of messages from people who'd heard my speech. They were all really complimentary and I thought that would be the end of it. What was to follow was completely unexpected. It probably wouldn't have happened had a reporter not been visiting the school to interview the headmaster about something unrelated. Mr Hill asked me if I'd mind him mentioning my speech to her. It didn't worry me at all, although if I hadn't been focusing on the chemo, I probably would have said no. At most, I thought I might get a little thing on the Stuff news website or the top left-hand corner on page 12 of *The Press*. There ended up being a full article about me in *The Press* the next day, and then it got picked up by a couple of news websites. I thought that was my 15 minutes of fame, but it turns out I was wrong.

I don't really use Facebook as I'm quite a private person, so I didn't see it explode on social media. Jemima was with me at the hospital a couple of days later — she'd quite often spend hours a day just sitting with me when I was having chemo, which was pretty amazing — and she was checking her Facebook. She said, 'What?!! There's an article about you on *Nine News* in Australia and it's got 5000 likes on it!' It took a while for that number to sink in. But that was nothing. By the end of the day, a TV3 article in New Zealand had 50,000 likes and some 350,000 views.

I would lie there while Jemima played a game: refresh Facebook and see how many new stories there were about me. The stories were multiplying faster than my cancer had been. For someone who is as private as me, it was terrifying, completely surreal, and a little bit intoxicating. It's a situation that you can never imagine yourself experiencing. There I was in isolation and the world was coming to me.

The media went mental. TV3 wanted to interview me, TV One wanted me on *Breakfast*, the news and *Sunday*. We were so unprepared to deal with the attention that we just diverted it all back to my school. I sure couldn't deal with it and I didn't want my parents to have to. They told me they were more interested in me living than talking to the media. Mr Hill was fantastic and really took the heat for us. It took up a hell of a lot of his time dealing with the media, doing interviews and answering questions. We all appreciated what he did so we could just focus on what was happening with my health.

An Australian TV show wanted to do a live cross to me in hospital. It was the eighth day of my chemotherapy, I was in isolation, and still staring down the barrel of death — but they wanted to do a live cross. It was kind of hilarious.

The hospital handled the attention really well. During my time there, the ward received dozens of calls from media outlets asking to speak to me, sometimes being deceptive about who they claimed to be. There were even some reporters who would call the hospital pretending to be related to me. None of these calls were put through to my room. The hospital staff looked after me like I was one of their own family.

When I had been in AMAU and short of reading material, I'd checked out the emergency planning book the staff had on the wall. It had what to do in case of fire, tsunami, power cuts, armed intruders, bomb threats . . . and media intrusion. I thought that was pretty weird, but decided it must have been for when they had famous people in hospital. I never imagined that a week later they'd need it because I was there.

It took a few more days before the story hit the media outside of New Zealand and Australia. But before long my story was being reported in *Time*, *The Washington Post*, *The Huffington Post*, *The New York Times*, *Cosmopolitan*,

The Daily Mail and *The Guardian*. There was even an article about me on *UniLad*, which said of my speech, 'It really is emotional to watch, and you have to consider the fact that Jake not only knows he could well die while actually making the speech, but that his classmates are also going to be seriously affected.' I thought that was hilariously untrue. That would have been a great look for the school if I'd died on stage!

A lot of the articles were saying that I had terminal cancer, and that was the first time a lot of people I knew had even heard about me being sick. Even some of my mates took a lot of convincing that I was planning to live through this, all going well.

It occurred to me that the media might be less interested in me living than delivering a good story. Some may have been enticed to read the story by the sadness of seeing an 18-year-old guy who might die. My speech was passably motivating, but I realise it wouldn't have had the same impact were it not for the circumstances I found myself in. It really was the epitome of 'clickbait' — you would be hard-pressed to write a story more enticing in a grim kind of way.

The school put the video of my speech up on YouTube and the views steadily climbed to around 1.7 million. But that doesn't take into account all the people who saw it on news sites that had ripped it from YouTube. The real viewership is probably something like 20 million.

NEVER READ THE COMMENTS

Along with the media attention came the inevitable comments from those who believed they knew exactly what was needed to cure me. I bet they never imagined that I would actually be lying in my hospital bed reading what they were saying. Some of the comments were absolutely hilarious. I needed to eat baking soda. I needed to rub olive oil and molasses on the places the tumours were — in my case that would be a full-body marinade. I needed to smoke marijuana (for medicinal reasons, of course . . .). Another message I got said, 'Marimbrimo, good evening Jake. I hope that you be good. If the permits can I help you. I saw your talk to college. Today cures have been advanced but also want to suggest this. To drink half a kilogram of squeezed carrot juice every day.' I had enough problems without turning orange.

Along with the so-called experts came the trolls. One of my favourites was, 'This is cancer to my eyes.' Followed up with: 'Damn bruther wrote dis. He only 8. He don't mean it tho.'

A page called Hope for Nigeria commented on the video: 'A brave guy. He has a strong Nigerian spirit.' It was the first I'd heard of it!

Then someone said, 'Good job. Can I have your cancer please? I'm sick and tired of living and am too much of a coward for suicide but I'm done with the insanities of my life.' That sort of thing was pretty hard to deal with.

A stranger started a Facebook page in my name that

quickly gained 5000 followers. Then the guy started posting things pretending to be me. Thankfully, he didn't post anything bad but it was still fake. We had to go through the police to get it shut down.

Later, when John Key wore one of my wristbands, he got so much hate for it. They were made as a fundraiser, and they had, 'Be gallant, be great, be gracious, and be grateful' written on them. Nic Hill saw the prime minister at a function and he gave him one. The next day, a photograph of John Key wearing it was on the front page of *The Press*, saying that the prime minister was supporting me. Cue the haters. 'John Key's using this poor kid with cancer to try and get publicity.' It wasn't like that at all — I thought that it was amazing that he wanted to share my message. Besides which, I'm pretty sure being prime minister gave him plenty of publicity already.

PEOPLE ARE PRETTY AMAZING

In the aftermath of the speech, I got about 1500 emails from all over the world. No one had my email address so they just sent messages to my school. Nic Hill walked into my hospital room one day with several boxes overflowing with reams and reams of paper. His executive assistant had printed them all out for me to read. I don't want to think about all the extra work I had created for her. The school was just about to head into exams, and every time they refreshed their email there'd be another 60 messages addressed to me. Never mind what it must have done to their printing budget!

I also felt pretty guilty about the presents that arrived. I got lots of new pairs of pyjamas. Someone bought me a Swanndri hat — my school colours were blue and black, and I used to wear a blue and black-checked Swanndri — so I got the matching hat to cover up my bald head when the time came for my hair to fall out. Josh McKay, who was the captain of the first XV and a super nice guy, gave me a beanie that he'd got playing for the New Zealand Schools rugby team. That really meant a lot to me.

At that point, some people suggested I set up a Givealittle page, but it didn't feel right. I had all the treatment I needed for free. Nevertheless, it didn't stop some people dropping money at the school. Some donated money they found on the ground. There is a generous Christchurch librarian out there who gave me $1000 'to buy myself an ice cream'.

There were funny t-shirts and a tissue box with my individual school photos like mugshots of me on the outside. The Old Boys gifted me an Old Boy tie and continued to visit with fresh scones and muffins on a regular basis. The bar I had been working at, and two of my friends' mothers, donated money for wristbands. My parents were also shown immense kindness by family, friends, and the staff and parents at the schools my half-siblings go to. Their freezers were quickly full. Like me, they found the kindness overwhelming.

The blankets I got were the best things. Because I'd lost

so much weight, the starched hospital sheets felt scratchy and I got cold really easily, so having a ready supply of blankets was a real treat.

I got handwritten letters from the prime minister and the governor general wishing me well. Dan Carter sent me a signed copy of his book. I got about 300 cards — some from people I knew, but many from people I'd never met. Every single one was as special as the last one, as they all meant that someone had taken time out of their day to choose a card, then sit down and write to me, and figure out where to send it. It meant so much to me and gave me real strength. Whenever I felt bad or low, I'd sit there and read the cards and letters from people who really wanted me to live. That was powerful.

> Don't ask someone going through chemo if there's anything they want you to bring them. Making decisions is hard enough, and it just adds more responsibility that they don't need. If you really want to bring them something they'll use (and this goes for anyone in hospital for more than a couple of days), bring them a brand-new, soft, cuddly blanket.

I got notes from people saying that I gave them strength to face whatever they were going through. That was amazing, too. I got messages from three separate people who had been suffering from depression, who told me the speech snapped them out of it. A lot of people who had

Burkitt's got in touch. That was great as I knew that they understood what I was going through, and I also knew that they'd survived it.

I got sent beanies from all around the world. Even though you watch the news and there's so much terrible stuff going on, I feel fine because I know what the world is really like and that there are some pretty amazing people out there.

I still meet people now who tell me that they have been praying for me ever since I got diagnosed. Some are still wearing my wristbands.

One of the coolest things I got sent was a photo from the Christchurch Police Armed Offenders' Squad. They were all in their AOS gear, including big guns, holding a sign that said, 'Fight hard, Jake. The Christchurch Armed Offenders' Squad are right behind you.' How cool is that?

> If you're thinking about doing something nice for someone — do it. You never know how much it might change their life. And if it doesn't, at least you tried.

Day 10 of chemotherapy
Dear Jake

And finally we are in double figures, day 10. I remember how excited you were to turn 10 years old because it was double figures, and then 13 because it meant you were a teen, and then 16 (you and I bunked school and took you for your driver's license, looked into your firearms license and signed you up to give blood).

I know you are busy with all that is going on, and struggling to get through these so I will keep today's super-brief.

Gratitude oozing today because:
1. Hell's Pizza and Argie Bargie (yes I know it is not really spelt like that — blame Nana!) gloved up and made food super hygienic for you (with pride) which you ate up.
2. You tolerated the drug you had a severe shaking/chilled reaction to this time last week, and also 24 hours of chemo.
3. You ended up on antibiotics (like in my dream last night) but the infections appear manageable.
4. You are in better spirits today and ate more than yesterday.
5. Going viral globally hasn't changed you. But you still haven't done the dishes yet. They keep saying your parents must be so proud of you. How can I be proud when the dishes are piling up back here . . .?

I am so sorry this is happening to you. But I'm pleased the secret is out. You know, that you're f&%$ing amazing. x

6 | FOOD IS NOT JUST FUEL

Food was a real mission for me the whole time I was in hospital. So much so that my parents would celebrate a little bit every time I felt like eating anything. To start with, I couldn't eat because my mouth was so full of tumours that it hurt when I would chew. Never mind that I'd just had two of my wisdom teeth out! The hospital had a special diet for people who couldn't handle solids — it was mostly jelly and porridge, I think. Every now and then I'd try to eat something with a bit more substance to it, and it never worked out well. Chewing little bits of toast was an endurance event. All I wanted was a piece of Marmite toast, but it hurt like hell.

A week into chemo and I got the news that my gum cancer was all gone. I was looking forward to eating being a bit more comfortable. It was, but the chemo made me feel sick sometimes, so I still didn't want to eat because I constantly felt like throwing up.

One day, not long into the treatment, I decided I really wanted lasagne. Mum went out but I told her not to get me any because I didn't want to put her to any trouble. The next thing I know, Georgia arrives in my room with a plate of lasagne. I asked her where it had come from and she pretended that she'd just happened to find it in the fridge, when of course Mum had gone out to buy it specially. I managed to get some of it down and keep it there.

Speaking of lasagne, another night when Dad was visiting me during chemo, we watched something about Garfield on TV. I hadn't been feeling very well but had been holding it together. That was until Dad decided to mention Garfield's favourite food — lasagne. All I could think of was a big slice of steaming hot cheesy lasagne and — WHOOSH — I was violently throwing up. Dad never talked about food in the hospital again.

> Don't talk about food with someone who is
> having chemo unless they mention it first.
> Vomiting is a likely consequence if you do.

I had to be careful with food that hadn't been prepared by people I knew, and cabinet food was out of the question.

I was pretty much on the pregnancy diet. I couldn't eat soft cheeses, preserved meats, anything that potentially could have bad bacteria in it. I could really only eat food that was cooked fresh by someone who knew what they were doing.

I wasn't really meant to have takeaways, but there were a couple of places — Hell Pizza and Arjee Bhajee (an Indian restaurant that is a Christchurch institution) — that would make sure the food was prepared in a super-hygienic way just for me. That was pretty amazing.

One of the things I did crave while I was in hospital was enchiladas — and these days I can't even look at them. It's the same with fish and chips. The smell of them makes me feel sick. Nachos were another favourite that I can't stand now.

At one point, I got within half a kilo of having to have a feeding tube up my nose and into my stomach, so I had four weeks where I ate McDonald's every morning just so I could gain weight. I'd eat 1500 calories for breakfast each day and that kept the feeding tube at bay. On the days my parents weren't able to bring McDonald's, my grandparents would. That was so helpful in keeping my weight up.

Towards the end of my treatment, I'd eat the weirdest stuff. One day I ate a kilo of potato salad, then drank a litre of grapefruit juice. I followed that up with four ice creams. I pretty much ate whatever I felt like as long as I could get it in and keep it down.

Every single meal was preceded by as many ice creams

as I could eat. I'd eat four Trumpets and feel really pleased with myself, instead of terribly guilty! I could also get through as much grapefruit juice as you could bring me. I'd consume three times my recommended daily sugar intake in grapefruit juice alone. I thought I'd get in trouble, but the doctors told me to go for it. I didn't need telling twice.

During 100 or so nights in hospital, I probably ate the food they provided only three times, apart from breakfast, which was just toast, so pretty hard to stuff up. Mum and Dad worked as a team and took turns to bring in three meals a day.

The lunch lady was lovely and I'd feel guilty that she'd come to pick up my food and it would never have been touched. The menu used to appear in two-week cycles, so once you've been there for a while, you know what to expect the next day. It's a very different experience being in hospital for three days to have your appendix out, compared to being in there for three months when your appetite is really limited anyway.

I was lucky that my family could bring food in for me. I feel really sorry for people who don't have that luxury. I understand that it is not easy to produce food for so many people, and that the hospital has to work to a budget. I understand that the people on the ground are trying their best, but good food is such a big part of your recovery.

Chemo really messes with your appetite and your taste buds, so what you want to eat and what you can eat varies. If you take food to a patient and they end up giving it to their visitors and the nurses, don't feel deflated. You have still done a good deed by feeding the support crew!

7 | HOPE IT'S TERMINAL

LAUGHTER IS THE BEST MEDICINE — OR MAYBE THE SECOND BEST AFTER CHEMO

Within a week of making the speech at my school prizegiving, my body was in neutropenia. Basically, that means that you have no immune system. I had pretty much no neutrophils — a type of white blood cell — in my body. The white blood cells are the ones that fight infection, and being neutropenic meant that if an infection had been introduced to my body, it would mount no defense whatsoever. While I was in that stage, there was no leaving my hospital room without a big filtered mask on, not many visitors, no touching, and definitely no sick people.

I was never bored when I was in hospital. I spent a lot of time on my phone and watching TV. I had an Xbox in there but I only played it once. I managed to fill hours and hours. I even managed to put a few bets on at the TAB.

I joked about how once I got cancer, I'd used up all my bad luck. When Cup Day — the New Zealand Trotting Cup is a huge event in Christchurch — rolled around, I drew a horse called Arden Rooney in Mum's work sweepstake. I figured I might as well back it at the TAB, too, so chucked quite a big bet on it. It's funny how when you're lying in bed possibly dying of cancer, money doesn't have quite as much meaning as it previously had. Arden Rooney won and I made a very tidy profit. Now I think of it, I never lost a single bet the whole time I was in hospital. Maybe there was something in it . . .

The internet gave me a vital link to the outside world. It meant that I could maintain contact with my mates, have plenty of banter and stay in the loop via group chat messages. I never felt lonely because I was always connected to my friends, even though I couldn't leave my room.

> Don't put any pressure on someone who is sick to keep in contact with you. The best messages I got were the ones that finished with, 'Don't feel you need to reply to this.'

My friends dealt with my illness really well, all things considered. Only on very few occasions did I feel that I was treated differently by them after my diagnosis, and this was really important to me. The word 'cancer' has such a stigma attached to it but, after I had made a few jokes about it, my mates understood that they didn't have to take it all so seriously because I didn't. My diagnosis didn't make me safe from a roasting in a group chat, or from a bit of banter with the lads about me having no hair, and this was really important to me.

One of my friends even went to the trouble of writing me a poem. It read:

> 'Hold
> on,
> pain
> ends.
> Ignore
> the
> sorrow,
> the
> errors,
> regrets
> made.
> Inspire
> nations,
> appreciate
> life.'

Which is a pretty decent poem, until you read the first letter of each word. Got it? The hidden message is, 'Hope it's terminal'.

I found that poem so funny that I wrote it up on the whiteboard in my hospital room. Some people were horrified, but I loved it — it was such a relief to me to joke about the situation instead of being grim. I didn't want anything more in my life to change than already had, especially not involving my friends.

> If someone you know is going through cancer
> (or any other big upheaval), don't treat them
> any differently. They've already gone through so
> much change, the last thing they need is for the
> people closest to them to alter the way they
> treat them.

Speaking of my friends, a few of them had a knack of coming to visit and staying a little too long. They'd show up, stay for two hours because they'd have nothing to do, and muck around with everything in the room. Some days, I'd have to pretend I was asleep or subtly buzz the nurses to make them leave. I didn't want to tell them to leave, but at the same time I didn't want to throw up on myself while they were there.

> Don't stay in a hospital room for more than
> 15 minutes when you visit someone, unless they
> ask you to.

That said, there were times when I was really glad to see visitors. I was grateful for my Auntie Leanne and my cousins Amera and Janna, who travelled from Wellington. My Great-Auntie Julie, who was also being treated for cancer, would sometimes pop in and we would talk about anti-nausea meds and share our funny treatment tales. A couple of family friends helped entertain all of us when our conversations were drying up. My mother's friend, Emma, brought in a 1960s *Playboy* magazine. It was the funniest gift I got and, even though the women were more modestly dressed than those in today's music videos, I was terrified a nurse would find it and think it was my reading material of choice.

Then there was the day an unknown visitor popped in. A woman showed up wanting to see me and hand over a gift. Mum said, 'No, sorry, he's not taking visitors right now. But I'm his mum and I'll give it to him. Thank you.' They had a bit of a chat and Mum left. The woman stayed around and when the nurse had her back turned, she snuck into my room. She came and sat at the end of my bed and was talking to me as if she knew me. I was just really confused and wasn't sure what to do. Thankfully, I had five members of the school's first XV with me at the time who were all looking at me, waiting for the nod to tackle and carry her out. At that moment, one of the nurses walked past and caught my eye. She came in and made sure that my unwanted visitor was escorted out of the hospital. The lady then started phoning, sometimes twice a day, to check on me and asking to be put through. I so appreciate the effort that the nurses and the hospital staff on the front line made to protect me from unwanted intrusions. They weren't trained to be someone's bodyguard, but they did a fantastic job at it.

My treatment continued through visits, although blood transfusions often made visitors feel a little squeamish. I remember the first time I was given a transfusion. The nurse brought the bag of blood into my room, hooked it up and attached it to my arm. Dad was sitting in a chair across the room. We locked eyes. He looked worried. 'What if that bag of blood has come from someone from Christ's College?' We both just cracked up. Every time after that, I used to try to work out whether I'd rather have blood from someone from Christ's College, from St Bede's or from Shirley Boys' High — all rival schools of mine!

> Sign up to be a blood donor. You never know when you are going to need bags and bags of the stuff. I'd been a donor, but I'd only given blood three times. The third time I went, I decked it and they wouldn't let me back! Still, that's better than none, I guess. Unfortunately, my cancer rules me out from ever being able to donate again.

8 | WELL, BODY, YOU TRIED TO KILL ME

YOU CAN PUT A POSITIVE SPIN ON ANYTHING IF YOU REALLY TRY

Twelve days into chemo, a mark under my eye began worsening so I had a CT scan, which showed there was no cancer left in my face. That was pretty bloody amazing. Given the cancer in my face had been growing so fast, the fact that it had gone was a good indicator that the rest of the cancer in my body was probably gone as well. That same day I had another big win — it was the first time in four weeks that I'd been able to sit up in bed. Up until then, I'd been so weak that I couldn't handle that much exertion. And when I say 'sit up', it was with the back of the bed raised up to support me. The nurses used to say that I should be spending at least 15 minutes a day sitting up in a chair or in bed. And I'd say, 'How am I supposed to do that? How is that possible?' On day 12, it finally became possible and, even though it was exhausting, it felt really good.

I had an ensuite bathroom attached to my room, so I'd manage to drag myself in there when I needed to go to the toilet. I'd have to pee into bottles and place them aside for the nurses. It was all very technical — they'd measure how much I was drinking and they'd measure how much I was peeing out.

There were times when I wondered why I had to bother with going to the bathroom, when I could have just peed in a bottle while I was in bed, but it was all part of keeping me mobile and stopping my muscles from seizing up. Lying in bed for days on end, your body loses conditioning — I could only lie on my back or my stomach, because I had lost so much weight that lying on my side made my hip bones press into the mattress. If I did lie on my side, I had to have a pillow between my legs to stop them knocking together.

I reached the point where, whenever I got out of bed, I'd make my parents look the other way because I didn't want them to see what I'd become. When my nana was dying of cancer, she wouldn't let people see her as she was wasting down to 33 kilograms, and now I understood why.

One night, I got out of bed when all my family had

gone home. I hobbled over to the mirror at the side of my bed and, just wearing my undies and a singlet, I looked at my reflection in the mirror. I could see my ribcage, my arms stuck out at funny angles, my shoulders poked right out, and my legs were bowed and so thin I could wrap my thumb and forefinger around my calf. I know it sounds quite crude, but the only thing I can compare it to was the pictures I'd seen of people in prisoner-of-war camps. I felt a disconnect between me and my body. All I could think was that it had been absolutely pillaged by cancer, completely destroyed, messed up beyond all recognition and mutilated beyond my very belief. I laughed and thought, 'Well, body, you tried to kill me, but I've well and truly got you back for it!'

That disconnect continued for a long time. Every time I'd look in a mirror it wasn't me I saw looking back. That skinny person — and later, that person with no hair, no eyebrows, no eyelashes — wasn't me. It didn't look like the person I pictured inside my head as being me.

It was around this time that I realised some people can use their bodies to walk on the moon; others can run marathons. Some people have bodies that can trek to the South Pole, swim across huge stretches of water, or base jump from cliffs. Meanwhile, I couldn't even get to 19 without my body trying to kill me!

I had a physio who would come and see me every couple of days to make me do exercises to keep my muscles toned. I developed a really good technique of pretending to be asleep when they arrived.

It was around this time that we had some good news, too, as my kidneys had come back online and started functioning properly again. That was a relief to me, but probably more so for the members of my family who had been lining up to be donors if I had needed a kidney transplant.

THANKS, BUT I'D RATHER YOU DIDN'T VISIT ME TODAY

Speaking of family, I was grateful that it was me going through this because I wouldn't have wanted to watch someone I loved suffering. I reckon it was easier for me than it was for my family and Jemima. I don't know how I would have coped if I'd had to watch any of them suffer, and I maintain they all had it tougher than I ever did.

My parents spent a *lot* of time with me when I was in hospital. As a result, we grew much closer. Mum and I got to the point where we'd say the same things at the same time. We'd talked about pretty much everything there was to talk about, and sometimes she would unwittingly repeat herself. Finally, our conversations would just descend into silliness. One day, a nurse walked in to hear me tell Mum to shut up. She replied, 'No, you shut up.' My response was, 'No, you shut up.' And so it went for a bit. It must have sounded awful to anyone else, but because there was no menace behind it, we both found it completely hilarious and surprisingly cathartic.

Not many guys my age will have spent as much time with their parents as I did during my time in hospital. Sit in a room with anyone for six to 12 hours a day, with nothing much to do, for weeks on end, and you'll begin to get sick of them very quickly.

Mum says I was never mean or bitter to anyone, but I spent a lot of time trying really hard not to be. That was a real lesson in saying things in my head rather than out loud. I also learnt to tell people what I needed. Like, I just need to be on my own for a bit. I even had to tell some people I really liked that I'd prefer it if they didn't visit. It was not a reflection on them, but about how much energy I had and how I was choosing to expend it.

At times when the battle is exhausting, visitors unintentionally take more energy than they return. They also unintentionally bring their own issues into the room, be it memories of their hospital stays, or people they love dying, or their inability to come to terms with the fear they may lose you. Sometimes they feel guilty and try to overcompensate by making their life sound terrible. But, seriously, when you are facing death, hearing someone complain about their flat tyre, a difficult work colleague or how busy they are, has just the opposite effect.

One thing I realised very quickly was that sympathy can be overpowering — in the same way that getting a lot of presents is overwhelming. Each person's expression of sympathy comes with an expectation that you should acknowledge and reply to them, usually by playing it down and reassuring them ('I'll be fine, don't worry

Showing some school pride at
one of my football games.

The night of my school formal — four months before I was diagnosed.

In front of Christchurch Boys' High at the ANZAC service in 2015.

Being a teenager early one morning in Auckland.

With my principal, Nic Hill, during the standing ovation before I gave my end-of-year speech.

The boys doing the school haka for me. Absolutely the most humbling and powerful thing I've ever experienced.

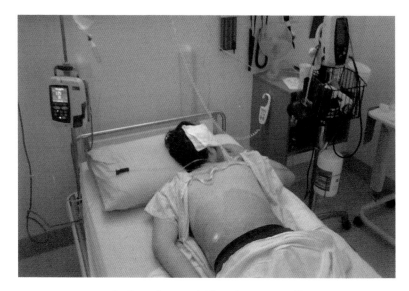

Just after my kidney biopsy. I still
hadn't come around yet.

With Auntie Leanne
and one of my nurses
the night I went on my
adventure to the vending
machines, complete with
CBHS tie and first XV cap.
Check out how skinny my
ankles and calves are!

How I spent a good portion of my time in hospital.

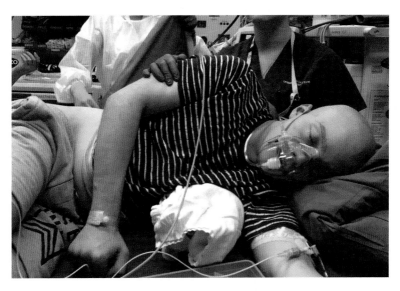

Knocked out for my (hopefully) last ever bone marrow aspirate.

Having my distinct lack of eyebrows remedied before a day of TV interviews.

Working hard at the Burwood Spinal Unit.

Celebrating with Uncle Steve and mum the night I was told I was in remission.

Two days before Jemima left for Aussie. My eyebrows were finally coming back. Stoked!

Recording a voiceover for Māia Health Foundation about two months into remission.

In Auckland giving another speech, this time for a charity fundraising dinner.

about me'). Sometimes sympathy can focus more on the person giving it — they are showing their reaction to your situation. It then falls to you to comfort them, when their initial intention was to try and comfort you!

This is something the hospital staff are amazing at. They've had enough experience and have spent enough time with patients to know that the last thing I needed was more sympathy. That's not to say they weren't caring or kind with me, but they weren't in my face with sympathy. The very first time I arrived at the BMTU, just a day after being diagnosed with stage 4 cancer, the nurse who greeted me apologised for something. My situation? No — she apologised for the hideously bright green La-Z-Boy chair in my hospital room. That humour was just what I needed.

My relationship with Jem was strengthened by the time we spent together in hospital. We became so close in such a short period. Even though she had her end-of-year exams and athletics, she still managed to make spending time with me a priority. We'd only been dating for a short while, but the process had been accelerated for us by a combination of pain, adversity, fear, and intensive periods of time together in a situation neither of us could have foreseen.

Even though we were super close because of my being in hospital, there was one thing I didn't want Jem to have to deal with — my hair falling out. I'd been having chemo for two weeks by this point, and I'd wake up every morning and check if my hair was still attached. On day 14, I found out it wasn't. I tugged at a bit and it just came out by the handful. And it wasn't just the hair on my head that was falling out. All my body hair did, too. I've got really hairy legs, so every time I moved in bed, there'd be more hair on the sheets. To speed the process up, I would just lie there and pull it out by the handful and put it in the rubbish bin beside my bed. But when I knew Jem was coming in, I'd get Mum to help me get up and we'd sweep all the hair off the sheets so that she didn't have to lie in it if she climbed into bed to watch TV with me!

I met another person while I was in hospital who was a few years older than me and had been diagnosed with Burkitt's about two weeks before me. His was the first case they'd seen in Christchurch in years. It's that rare. Weirdly, there was another case shortly after me, and another two after that. Five cases in five months. I have met three of the other Burkitt's sufferers and our mums keep in touch.

Day 15 of chemotherapy
Dear Jake

I felt extra sad for you today. You said you hadn't felt this bad since when you were first admitted to hospital. They are still pumping you with two types of antibiotics. Mouth ulcers. And on top of all that, it was you and me for 12 hours straight (your Dad in Auckland and Jem in Dunedin). I find me boring, what the hell must it be like for you?

I joked (that first time you went into A&E when you

were vomiting blood 3.5 weeks ago) that over the time you've been sick, we've discussed everything. We've gone past that to a whole new grunting at each other level since then.

Today you had handfuls of hair coming out. Well, that was a surprising first.

When you slept you twitched to the point you woke yourself up. I was worried you were moving into a seizure.

We laughed today about that NCEA deciphering mental/unfamiliar poetry/text question and, after hours of you not being yourself, it was a relief to see you smile.

Dancing on gratitude tables, because:
1. You will have other visitors than me to entertain you tomorrow.
2. Those two anti-nausea meds together worked well enough to get noodles and tuna in you tonight.
3. Josh McKay gifted you a first XV beanie to pop on your freshly shaved head. (Sheryl should be shaving it in the morning.)
4. The night nurse is doing reiki on you. Not quite chemo but why not!
5. I met another mum in the family room who was

great to talk to (her son has Burkitt's, and is about a cycle ahead of you).

I love you, you love me, we're a happy family . . . okay, this is stupid. When a purple dinosaur starts singing in my head I know it's time for bed.

Love from your Mar-yar (what you called me when you were four). x

SOMETIMES YOU HAVE TO STAND YOUR GROUND (EVEN IF YOU CAN'T ACTUALLY STAND)

There was a clot in my arm so the pump wasn't able to push the treatment into me like it normally would. This meant that the alarm on the pump kept going off. Every time the alarm went off, I'd have to roll over, turn it off and press a button to start it again. It was driving me nuts. After a few goes at that, I lashed out and punched the machine. That was probably a low point for me. Mum was a bit worried that I might be the first-ever seriously sick person to get evicted from the hospital on account of violence against a piece of malfunctioning machinery!

As a result of the blood clot, my PICC line had become infected and had to be removed. I was neutropenic at the time, so I had zero immune response. This also meant that there was a possibility that a *Staph* infection that I'd picked up earlier might have travelled to my heart, kidneys and lungs. If it had, I would require immediate surgery to save my life, so that meant a bunch more tests for me. It also meant that they had to take my PICC line out and replace it, a procedure that wasn't a whole lot of fun.

To start with, a staff member told me that the PICC would have to be replaced with a CICC — a centrally inserted central catheter. This would have been a more complex procedure, and the line would have to go straight into my jugular vein. I just wanted another PICC line put in, but on my other arm, and I said as much. I stood my ground and she walked out of the room, saying that she would come and see my new CICC line the next day. That annoyed me a bit and I called out that that wouldn't be happening, because I wouldn't sign the paperwork to allow them to do so. The whole encounter was really unusual, as most of the staff really listened and considered my opinion when it came to different procedures. When I reflect, I guess it was important to me to have some power over the decisions about what was happening to me, where possible. I didn't want any of this to happen to me, but if I could have a say about something that was going to happen to my body, I was grateful when the staff considered my opinion.

When the duty haematologist came in to see me later that day, it was agreed to try a second PICC line. Not only was the line successfully inserted in my other arm, I may also have got a little bit of a smug smile that said, 'I told you so' when I saw that nurse the following day.

A HOSPITAL CAN QUICKLY AND UNEXPECTEDLY BECOME YOUR SAFE PLACE

The last time I had left hospital was the night I made my speech. Since then, I hadn't been outside at all, and had become really comfortable with staying indoors. There was a psychologist working in the background with the nurses and my parents. They were worried because I wouldn't go out. It didn't bother me, but they were really concerned about it. I saw hospital as my safe place. The BMTU was my sanctuary, where I had no responsibilities. I never had to worry about anything other than getting better while I was there — everything I needed was attended to. If I felt sick, I'd ring a bell and anti-nausea medication would appear. If something started going wrong with my body, a team of highly skilled professionals would nut-out how to help me. There was no pressure on me at all.

The day before my first round of chemo ended, the psychologist persuaded me to go on an outing to Hagley Park, just opposite the hospital. I hated it.

Mum and Dad wheeled me across the road to the park in a wheelchair. The last time I'd been to that park was with Jemima about a month earlier, before I had been diagnosed. Going back made me realise how much things had changed in a really short time, and I didn't want to think about that. It was like mixing my two worlds together — the one before cancer and the one with cancer — and I wouldn't have done that at all if I wasn't made to. I wouldn't have left the hospital at all if I'd had it my way.

While we were sitting in the park, Mum said something like, 'Oh, this is quite nice.' I replied, 'I fucking hate it.' And we sat there in silence for a while. Then Mum said, 'Do you want me to take you back?' To which I responded, 'Yes.'

I was in a wheelchair with my beanie on and a mask over my face. It was the middle of summer. I looked sick. People stared at me — I could see pity and fear in their eyes. I was that kid you see in public who you try not to stare at. I'd never pictured myself being 'that kid' — the kid who got cancer. How could I be the kid that got cancer?

Cancer was something that happened to old people, and sometimes to the most unlucky kids on the planet, which is why I always took my gold coin for CanTeen on mufti day. I had helped nurse my beloved Nana through her cancer to her death. That was where cancer should have stopped in my mind. Then all of a sudden, I became one of those unlucky kids. And I didn't want people to look at me like that.

Day 21 of chemotherapy
Dear Jake

Hooray!! End of round 1!!

It was hard to see the impact being outside had on you yesterday. I can't imagine what it must be like. I am really proud of how you are handling things. It seems you are already able to just sit with emotions like anger and sadness and not be freaked out by them or try and escape them — something I am still learning to do.

It was amazing to read all your fan mail yesterday. Wow, you have moved people. With your new mates John Key, Dan Carter and Sir Jerry Mataparae all writing to you. That letter that made you laugh was fantastic, the fan who wrote in a poetic manner and said, 'I'm the brother you never had'. I also liked the one from the teenage girl who was writing to you instead of studying. The prayer hankie. Five bibles. The old couple similar to Elaine and Mal. And Thomas from the UK sending you $250.

Today Lily caught something (a bird? mouse?). I could hear her outside. After she brought one in a couple of days ago (and proceeded to play with it) I locked the cat flap until it was done. She is in now looking pretty pleased with herself.

High-fiving complete strangers and cats because:
1. The needle went into your spine first time.
2. A new PICC line.
3. More food, flowers and cards.
4. You having courage to turn visitors away — great self-management.
5. Your appetite.

Love you, handsome. Mum xx

9 | CHEMO IS KIND OF BORING

Once I got into the rounds of chemotherapy, life became pretty mundane, with one day being much the same as the next. This is probably reflected in some of Mum's emails, which started to get a bit random at times.

End of round 1 of chemotherapy
Dear Jake

Here are the four funniest things I can think of since you've been in hospital:
1.   Snapping cross
A visiting chaplain loaned you her very special

cross, made out of wood from St Mark's Church before it was demolished. The cross (shaped like a capital T) is very dear to her. She prays with it half a dozen times daily, and hangs it from her robe when she delivers sermons. Because she was going to struggle to be away from it, she loaned it to you for a maximum of 12 to 24 hours. Unfortunately, someone put it in your hand when you were about to get your first lumbar puncture and you snapped it into two. I wasn't sure what you were going to say when you gave it back. 'Hi, where did you say you bought this from again?' 'Do you have any cellotape?' Or, 'Sorry, I'm not really the anti-Christ, despite how it may look!'

2. The male nurse

When they removed your sperm (like most times you got needled) they weren't successful, so you ended up with four needles in two testicles. Later, back in your hospital bed, you had to have a male nurse fondling your testicles (to ensure they hadn't blown up to the size of balloons). Leanne, you and I joked that next time you awoke he would be in your room fondling your testicles again, this time naked, claiming, 'Sorry, but we ran out of scrubs . . .'

3. Sam is brave

I received a lovely email. It was a very positive email, except that the whole way through she called you Sam. Sam is brave. Sam is strong. Sam will fight this.

4. The Legionnaire's. Funny, but not. Probably not actually, now I think about it.

Love you, you know it. x

The reference to Legionnaire's in Mum's message was down to the fact that even though I was in one of the most secure, germ-free places in the hospital, traces of Legionnaire's disease were found in the shower of my ensuite. Yep, a horrible and sometimes fatal bacteria was found hanging out in my shower. Because pretty much everyone on the ward was immuno-compromised, we all had to be put on doses of antibiotics as a precaution against the disease. Why the shower? *Legionella* bacteria loves a damp, warm environment, like plumbing or air-conditioning systems.

To the staff's credit, the bacteria was found and dealt with really quickly. That involved me shifting out of the room while they did a deep clean of the bathroom.

THE WORLD REALLY IS SMALL

In the time I was in hospital, I had heaps of staff members come and ask me if I was related to Dr Ross Bailey, my great-uncle whom I mentioned in my speech. It was everyone from receptionists, to admin people, to doctors and nurses who had worked alongside him.

One nurse was administering some medication, and

she asked me to read the details on my wristband. I said, 'Jakob Ross Bailey, 16 August 1997'. She stopped and said, 'Are you related to Dr Ross Bailey?' It was amazing to see the mark that he'd left on the place. He was a nephrologist — a kidney specialist. At the very start of the process, my grandparents and I joked about the fact that he would have killed me if my kidneys failed on me!

It was great to learn more about his life from people who had worked with him. He was a funny guy. He used to do red-pen marking on the student's work. One great example was: 'Thank you so much for documenting this patient's kidney failure for the last four days. It's a shame you didn't decide to do anything about it.'

NO ONE SHOULD BE DEFINED BY THEIR ILLNESS

There was still some fear that the blood clot in my arm would move to my heart. It was around the time that Jonah Lomu died of a heart attack, which was reportedly caused by a blood clot. That made my family worry even more. So when I got the news — on day 25 — that the clot wasn't travelling, meaning that it wasn't going to be in my lungs or heart any time soon, it was a massive relief.

To celebrate, I went for a walk to the vending machine. I was in a dressing gown that CanTeen had given me, a Christchurch Boys' High School Old Boys' tie and a CBHS first XV cap given to me by a man from Mum's work. Those caps are so treasured by their owners that I knew what a big deal it was for him to give it to me. He also wrote me an amazing letter that said, 'Jake, you were incredible before this and you're no different now.' The fact that someone could see that I wasn't being defined by my illness really meant a lot to me.

When I returned to my room, Mum conspired with me to pretend that I was asleep when the PICC nurse came to visit. Mum's fibs might have come back to bite her, as she got a really bad cold a couple of days later and couldn't come in to see me for a while.

While she was sick, I went neutropenic again. I was actually quite relieved, because when I wasn't neutropenic the hospital had the option of moving me out into a shared room. I hated the idea of sharing a room with people who were dying.

WHITE MEN WITH CANCER OF THE LYMPHATIC SYSTEM CAN'T JUMP

I found out that one of the nurses who was looking after me had had cancer when she was a teenager. As a result, she'd sustained nerve damage from badly performed intrathecal injections, which is when they inject stuff straight into the fluid surrounding the spinal cord. Some of my intrathecals had gone quite badly, and it was great to know that she was there looking after me. The nursing staff who cared for me were the most incredible people I've met in my life. They felt like family to me by the time

I left hospital — I still go back and visit them occasionally now just to catch up and see how they're doing.

A couple of days later, another nurse, Courtney, came in to see me before she started work. She wanted to show me her pretty out-there Christmas jersey, complete with pompoms. Never mind the fact that the temperature had been in the thirties in Christchurch that week! A lot of the nurses were in their early twenties, so I think they related a bit more to me because I was younger than most of the other patients in the unit. Whatever the reason, their visits really meant a lot to me.

I found interesting ways to keep myself entertained as the days stretched on. As a bit of a challenge, I decided to see how far off the ground I could jump. Given I had no leg muscles, it wasn't very far. My lack of jumping ability intrigued me. I had already climbed up on a chair the night before to check out just how wasted my calf muscles were. Once I got up there, I realised that my platelet count that day was almost nonexistent, and if I fell off I'd probably bleed out internally. I wouldn't even be able to reach the call bell. If I ruptured something, there was no way my blood would clot. Even though I was deathly ill, I was still a teenage boy who didn't really think through the consequences of my actions ahead of time. Luckily, I made it back onto the ground safely and was so exhausted by all the activity I had to lie down.

Also being exhausted was Mum's pool of ideas for things to talk about in her emails to me. As you can see from this little gem:

Day 35 (round 2, day 14 of chemotherapy)
Dear Jake

So pleased:
1. You now know white men can't jump (1980s thing you can google in your spare time). Although watching you trying to springboard off the ground was fun tonight.
2. You sat up heaps, smiled heaps, and gave me quotes to write to Leanne for the back cover of your inevitable future book and for the first time in a long time I saw a glimpse of the you you will be when we come through this. Awwwwww. Hence me turning from hugphobic to huggybear.
3. You didn't fall off the chair you climbed on to look at your calves in the mirror last night and haemorrhage everywhere (because your platelet count is low).
4. A nurse turned up wearing a seriously funky Xmas jersey tonight!

Lily is missing you. We are missing you. And I can hear you from here saying you are missing us too. Sorry, was that . . . you are missing beer too?

Love Mum x

THE WORLD IS PRETTY AMAZING

A really big moment for me came on 5 December, or day 36 of my treatment — I got to go home for a visit for the first time since 22 October. There was a back exit where you didn't have to go right through the hospital. It was really an emergency exit, but we used it as a shortcut to the car. I said goodbye to the nurses then I hobbled down there really slowly, insisting on carrying my own bag. There was no way I was going to let Dad carry it.

Nothing could have prepared me for the rush of emotions I felt as I stepped out of that door. I pushed it open to reveal a hot summer's day, the sound of birds chirping, the feeling of the sun on my face, and a light breeze. It was like walking into a wonderland.

Even though Hagley Park is right opposite the hospital, the thick windows of my room prevented me from hearing the usual sounds of the outside world. I'd been in hospital for over six weeks, and for nearly five weeks I hadn't heard birds chirping, I hadn't heard the wind rustling through the leaves on the trees. I hadn't even heard cars driving past. I hadn't felt fresh air on my face. I'd heard nothing but the constant hum of the air-conditioning unit and breathed nothing but filtered air. Walking out the door of the hospital, I went into what felt like sensory overload. The bright sunlight on my face, the breeze on my skin, and the sound of birds was incredible. It's completely impossible to describe. I've never felt anything like it before or since.

When I got into the car, I realised that I hadn't been in a car for five weeks. When in your life have you not been in a car for that long? Most people wouldn't go a single week without being in a car. I'd been lying still in a bed for so long that I almost had to learn again how a car moves. I couldn't get over how it seemed to glide over the road. All these things were coming past me and it felt so weird to be moving without doing anything.

Mum reckoned it was like taking me home from hospital the first time when I was a baby, she was so scared of breaking me.

Arriving home was both comforting and confusing in the sense that it hadn't changed at all. When I walked through the gate, it still squeaked like the last 1000 times I'd walked through it. The last time I'd heard it squeak, I was on my way to the maxillofacial surgeon. I had no idea that I wouldn't be home that night. I'd walked out thinking I was going to a routine appointment and I'd be back for dinner. I'd had no time to pack a bag or prepare myself for not coming home.

The last time I'd walked through that gate, I was 15kg heavier, I had hair, I didn't know I had cancer, I hadn't done my speech and no one knew who I was. Coming back through the gate, a month and a half later, I had cancer, I was halfway through chemo, my hair had fallen out, I'd made a speech that had gone viral, and the media were still writing stories about me. Despite all of that, my brother Harry was there to greet me with a big hug, the house still smelt like home and my room was just how I'd left it. It was so strange that so much had been changed, and yet stayed the same.

In hospital, I quickly got into the routine of the place. The nurses would do observations every four hours during the day, where they would take my temperature and my blood pressure. Overnight, they'd do it at midnight and then again at 6am. At midnight, I'd have all my tablets then sleep for six hours. Breakfast was dropped off at seven, the doctors would pop in and assess me at eight, and chemo would be hooked up at 8.30. Sometimes, I'd sleep through a lot of this and only really wake at about 10. There was always hustle and bustle. There was always someone to talk to — there'd be three nurses on all the time, so if my family weren't there and it wasn't too busy the nurses would come and sit with me and chat.

Going home, there was none of this. There were no constant interruptions to my day. When I went to bed, there was no one there for me to talk to. I know it sounds really weird but I missed it. I missed the security, I missed the predictability, I even missed the hum of the air-conditioning unit. I missed it so much that I couldn't sleep. That first night in my own bed, I didn't get to sleep until 5.30am — the time when I'd usually be waking for the first time if I was still in hospital.

When I got home, I weighed myself on the scales and I was stoked to find that I finally had a pretty low body-fat percentage when I measured my body mass index. For the first time in my life I had six per cent body fat. I was so stoked that I shared it with all my mates. 'Yes, guys!

I've dropped 15 kg and I'm in single digit body fat. It doesn't matter that it was cancer, but I did it!'

On my second day at home, we were all watching the news on TV, when I appeared as one of the top 10 quotes of the year. That was kind of weird. They showed some footage of me making my speech and I turned to Mum and said, 'Where's my hair gone?' She laughed.

SOMETIMES BEING AN ADULT IS GOOD

I'd have three nights at home and then I'd go back to the hospital during the day and receive my treatment in my room. When I went back into hospital after my first time at home, I got some really good news. I thought that I was nearly a third of the way through my chemo, but it turned out that I was almost halfway through. I only needed four rounds of chemo — not the six that had initially been prescribed.

I thought it might have been because I was healing really well, but it was actually because the specialists had revised the treatment protocol they were using. When you're under 18, they use a protocol designed for kids — six rounds. When you're over 18, they use an adult protocol of four rounds. Given I was 18 and three months, I kind of walked the line between being a child and an adult the whole time I was in hospital.

I was under the kids' register for anaesthetics, which meant that I could be given a general for some procedures that adults would have done under a local. This was especially good when it came to my intrathecals and some of the more invasive tests I had to have done.

When it came to deciding whether I should have four or six rounds, the haematologists consulted international experts on Burkitt's to make sure that I wouldn't be put at risk. I didn't know it, but at that stage I was starting to get nerve damage in my legs, which was caused by the chemo. Having fewer rounds meant there was likely to be less damage. In this case, I was quite happy to be treated like a grown-up.

While I was back in hospital in early December, I had one of my toughest nights in hospital. It was the night of Jem's school-leavers' ball. Two of my mates were dating two of Jem's friends so the three couples would all have gone together if I'd been well. While the others all went to the end-of-year event at St Margaret's, I was stuck in hospital. I saw photos of my name card on an empty seat and of the others having a great night. That was the first time I cried because I was angry about missing out on something due to the cancer. I put the blind down in my room so no one could see me, and beat the shit out of my pillow. I was so angry. I missed out on a lot of events at my own school, which sucked but it didn't upset me. Missing Jem's leavers' ball, though, made me feel like I was letting her down, and I hated that.

THINGS CAN CHANGE VERY FAST

On my fortieth day of chemo, Jem and I had a date night in hospital. Dad brought in a meal from Pedro's House of Lamb, so we could have dinner together. After we'd eaten, we went for a walk outside then spent some time exploring around the hospital. Back in the room, Jem climbed into bed with me and we watched Harry Potter movies until we fell asleep. It wasn't the most normal date I could imagine but it was still pretty amazing.

The next morning, I came back down to earth with a bump. One of the BMTU nurses came in and said, 'We need this room back today.' I asked if it would be okay if I could pack and get my dad to shift my stuff that afternoon, which they agreed to.

Then the nurse came back about five minutes later and said, 'Actually, we need you to pack up right now. We need it vacated as soon as possible so we can deep clean it before the next person comes in.' That panicked me a little bit. It was a strange way to find out that I was being discharged from hospital.

I'd been in the room for over a month. I had about 40 books I'd been given, I had boxes of printed emails, I had heaps of cards everywhere. On top of that there were my clothes and all the other stuff I'd needed while I was in hospital. It was a bit of a shock to be told I had to pack and get out, but I knew the next person in that room would be someone who needed it more than I did.

Mum had her end-of-year assembly at school and,

being the principal, she couldn't leave. Dad was in a meeting and Jem had gone to meet a friend for coffee. I felt absolutely shocking and had no idea how I was going to pack everything on my own. Thankfully, one of the cleaners and a nurse-aide came in and helped me. As well as all the boxes, I had seven big patient property bags full of gear, which I was then told I had to take with me. That was a bit confusing — I didn't have a car and I was barely capable of walking, let along carrying kilos and kilos of gear with me. In the end, they agreed to keep it in a staffroom so Dad could come and pick it all up later in the day.

I went and sat in the family room while I waited for Jem to arrive. When she got there, I told her what had happened and she took it in her stride. She went and got her car and we drove out to her parents' place in the country. It was a very strange way to meet my girlfriend's mother for the first time!

Luckily, her mum, Lisa, just gave me a big hug and said that she felt like she already knew me. I can't imagine what the whole process must have been like for them. One minute their daughter has this new boyfriend, and the next thing they hear he's in hospital, and then he's got cancer. Are you kidding me? What are the chances of that?

There was an odd parallel with Jem's parents. Her mum had had breast cancer not long after she met Jem's dad, and he had stuck with her throughout it. I guess that helped them to understand what Jem was doing with me.

Jem had saved a piece of brownie that she'd got at a café that morning. She offered it to me and even though

I had not been allowed to eat food from cafés, and a rich chocolate brownie was the last thing I felt like eating, I didn't feel like I could refuse. I wanted to be polite, so I took it and told her it was delicious. I explained the situation to her about two months later, and she said, 'Why didn't you tell me?'

HOME IS WHERE THE FOOD IS

My second day out of hospital was the halfway point in my chemotherapy. Apart from the days when my immune system crashed, I'd stay at home and just be driven to the hospital for my treatment. Mum called it 'drive-through' chemo. I liked that idea.

As a result of the blood clot in my arm, I was meant to learn to inject myself in the stomach with blood thinners, called clexane. They really hurt. The needle was tiny but the medicine stung badly. I hated doing it, so in the end I drove back to the hospital every day to get the nurses to do it! I constantly had a bad bruise on my belly from the injections, which had to be done every day for about a month. On some of those days, I had to have chemo anyway, so I was killing two birds with one stone when I went in to the hospital.

Even though I missed the security of being in hospital, there were a lot of benefits to being at home. One of them was that it was much easier for me to keep my weight up because I could eat whatever I wanted, whenever

I wanted. Like any typical teenager I could go to the pantry and graze whenever I felt like it. But the chemo really affected my appetite and I only ever ate what I could stomach. And sometimes that was a really weird combination of stuff. A typical day might include about two kilograms of potato salad with Nando's hot sauce, four or five ice creams, spinach and feta pie, 10 nectarines, with a litre of grapefruit juice to wash it down.

One of the other good things about being home was that I got to spend time with my eight-year-old brother Harry. The first time he saw me after I'd had my head shaved, he said to me, 'Oh, you look so good with your head shaved, Jake!' I don't know if that's what he really thought but he was super supportive of me. After I got home, he decided he wanted to have a matching hairdo so he got a number two shave all over. It was a seriously cute thing for a young kid to do.

On Monday 14 December, Jem and her family flew to Perth for Christmas. That was really tough for me as we'd been inseparable for so long; it was weird not having her around. The following day I was back at the hospital having an intrathecal as well as the usual intravenous chemo.

Day 46 (day 4, round 3 of chemotherapy)
Dear Jake

Thanks for a great big chat tonight. Was nice to talk about all our memories of this whole episode

(I refuse to call it a journey). Some hard times.
('Don't cry, Mum', 'Sniff, I'm not crying, see?').
Trying to work out if you have 'processed it' (what
does that look like?)

I hope these daily notes also serve as a useful
reminder of what was.

The song 'Sugar' (Robin Schulz) just came on
and we both agreed it reminds us of your time in
hospital those first few weeks. We've discussed all
the food you'll never be able to eat again including
McDonald's breakfasts and how long you've
potentially got until you can't stomach English
muffins and raspberry jam.

You had a general anaesthetic today, intrathecal
and intravenous chemo. The general anaesthetic for
intrathecal will be every Tuesday until the 19th.

I've ordered more wristbands and TradeMe are
coming to the party with no fees. They even put $50
into the account to start the ball rolling.

Thanking the big guy upstairs for:
1. Time sitting and talking with you.
2. You being on earth.
3. Your resilience. Despite bad chemo.
4. Jem's mum phoning me.

5. TradeMe coming to the party.

Hugs, Mum x

SOMETIMES YOU GET MORE THAN 15 MINUTES OF FAME

A couple of days later, I got the news that I'd won the Massey University 'Quote of the Year', which takes memorable quotes that are then voted for by New Zealanders. Apparently, I got about 70 per cent of the vote, but I think that might be because my family and extended family and their friends voted on every device they own! The quote that won was 'Here's the thing — none of us get out of life alive. So be gallant, be great, be gracious, and be grateful for the opportunities that you have.'

The other contenders were:

- 'I started here aged 27 in a suit I borrowed from my dad. I could never have dreamed what would happen in the next 24 years.' — John Campbell on the final *Campbell Live* show
- 'Squeaky sand, eh!' — Art Green after Poppy Salter farted on *The Bachelor*
- 'I survived The Kills!' — *X-Factor* contestant Joe Irvine
- 'Just my arm.' — All Blacks' coach Steve Hansen when asked what he had up his sleeve during the Rugby World Cup

- 'We've been asked to vote for the tallest dwarf.' — Marketing expert Mike Hutcheson on proposed new flag designs for New Zealand
- 'That's a very tantalising ponytail.' — Prime Minister John Key
- 'No man should have his wife's brain on his shirt.' — Philip Morgan QC at the Mark Lundy murder case retrial
- 'I used to make fun of him, I said no one could catch him because whenever the nostrils flared up he took all the oxygen.' — Eric Rush on All Black Jonah Lomu, who passed away in November that year
- 'The French love the coq.' — ACT Leader David Seymour during the debate whether to change the New Zealand flag.

I voted for Steve Hansen, who, when asked what he had up his sleeve in a media conference during the Rugby World Cup, replied, 'Just my arm.' Classic.

On the day the 'Quote of the Year' was to be announced, I was asleep with my phone charging next to me and was woken up by my phone vibrating non-stop. I knew straight away what it was — all my mates messaging me, giving me a hard time for winning. It was hilarious.

The funny thing about that quote is now when anyone uses the words 'gallant', 'gracious', 'great' or 'grateful' while I'm in the room, everyone turns and looks at me! If anyone starts the sentence with the words, 'Here's the thing . . .' I always butt in with 'none of us get out of life alive.' It makes for a good laugh.

SOMETIMES CANCER WORKS IN YOUR FAVOUR

The Saturday of that week marked two weeks since I'd been at home and doing drive-through chemo. That night was the first time I caught up with all my mates for a Christmas get-together. It was great to go out and have some fun and feel normal again. I'd put on a bit more weight and, apart from the beanie I was wearing, I looked kind of like myself again. They were all drinking and they quite liked that I couldn't because it meant that I'd drive them.

On another night out, when I was driving them home, we were stopped at a police checkpoint. I got breathalysed by one officer, then was stopped straight away by another one. I told him I'd already been tested and pointed back to the stop I'd just come from. He told me I had to do it again anyway, then breathalysed me. The police officer asked to see my licence, because I looked young and had passengers in the car. I pulled it out of my wallet and handed it to him. He stared at it for ages and then he stared hard at me. It was as if he thought the licence was fake. One of my mates, who was pretty drunk, leaned over and blurted out, 'He looks a bit different now. That photo was from before he had cancer!' The cop quietly handed my licence back and waved me on.

My family and Jem had previously noticed some

strangers recognise me when we were out, but it was around this point that I first started noticing it for myself — I'd been completely oblivious to it before. I realised that people didn't want to approach me because it would be really awkward if they came up and said, 'Are you that guy who's got cancer?' only to find out they were wrong!

10 | HAPPY (?) HOLIDAYS

IT DEFINITELY IS THE THOUGHT THAT COUNTS

The week before Christmas I had to go back into hospital, so Mum bought me a Santa suit to entertain the nurses. It was not just any Santa suit, though — it had tiny red velvet shorts with white fluffy bits on them and a skimpy tight top. I wore it into the hospital and had everyone in fits.

With the jokes all done, I was back on a 24-hour dose of chemotherapy. I had to take the pump with me whenever I went to the toilet or if I went for a walk, and being hooked up to it meant that I couldn't roll over in bed. It was so frustrating, especially after having had two weeks of the freedom of being at home. But that wasn't the end of it — after an entire day of getting the stuff pumped into me, I had to spend the next 48 hours on intravenous fluids to flush it back out. Not really the way I'd envisaged spending the week before Christmas, that's for sure.

One amazing thing about being in hospital just before Christmas was that people were so kind. The ward cleaner, who was a lovely lady, came in to see me and brought me a box of chocolates. When I was in hospital her smile used to brighten up my days every time I saw her. We'd chat a bit if I was feeling up to it and if I wasn't feeling well we didn't, but she had this lovely presence that just cheered me up. The fact that she'd thought of me at Christmas moved me so much.

Because I'd just had such a big dose of chemo, no one was sure if I'd be allowed to go home for Christmas. That, combined with Jem being in Perth with her family, meant it was a pretty bad time all around for me. I was feeling really down, but there was one little bright spot — a person from one of the cancer charities came in and said, 'I've got a Christmas present for you!' I was pretty excited to see what they'd got me. She handed over this big gift and said, 'Good luck getting home for Christmas Day, and I'll see you after Christmas!' Then she carried on with her rounds.

As soon as she left, I ripped into the parcel, paper flying everywhere. I was so excited. When I saw my gift I couldn't stop laughing — in the box was shampoo, conditioner and hair gel. Whoever donated that must not have realised it was going to someone having chemotherapy. I had not a single hair on my whole body — well, except for my eyebrows. This was enough to clean my eyebrows for life! I saw the funny side, although I do wish they'd just given me a nice pair of socks.

As it turned out, I got to go home a bit later that day. A mate in hospital wasn't so lucky. As I was packing my bag to leave he had to come back in because he had a high temperature. I felt bad for him and his family facing Christmas in hospital.

Day 55 (round 3, day 13 of chemotherapy)
Dear Jake

Santa brought you home for Xmas. Well, not literally, although Matt does appear to have a similar physique to the big fella.

Today you left hospital around lunchtime and took yourself back to hospital at 5pm for your stomach jab; you had lashings of cherries and blueberries; a parent from school dropped off flowers and a voucher and talked about her husband having Burkitt's; and you got Xmas carols stuck in your head due to my insistence to play a few during the ad breaks.

I haven't been as excited about Xmas for years and

it is simply because you are home. I feel blessed that you're here — not just home but alive. That was a close call.

Thanking my luck stars that:

1. You're home, even though your Santa outfit was brightening up the ward.
2. You've pretty much finished round three and you look the best you have in what feels like forever.
3. It has been two months since you went to hospital (Oct 22nd — it was a Thursday like today). Glad those two months are behind us.
4. We get to sing Christmas carols and see bunnies in Santa hats.
5. We've laughed a lot today.
6. You may never have to spend another night in hospital for your whole life — here's hoping.

Love always, Mum x

I ended up sleeping in until lunchtime on Christmas Day, then got up and did the usual festive stuff with the family — ate, talked and watched *Meet the Fockers*. While I was sitting there, I had moments when I could feel my heart beating in my spine. That was really weird. And it got us talking about how much had happened in the previous two months. Mum reckoned I never properly realised just how bad things had been when they were at their worst.

I think she was probably right. While I had dropped from 72kg down to 55kg in a matter of weeks, and I would hobble around hunched over like an old man, I never really thought about just how sick I was. I was always focused on getting better.

Jem got back from Perth the day after Boxing Day. It was so great to see her home. I took her out to dinner to a really nice Italian restaurant, Café Valentino, to celebrate. It was so great to go out and just do something normal as a couple. It was so hot that I even took my beanie off in the restaurant — and that hardly ever happened.

As I was leaving for dinner, Mum called out, 'See you, wouldn't want to be you!' I said, 'Why not?' Her reply was pretty cool. She said, 'Because I'm not as brave as you and I'd be scared of cancer.' Fair enough.

DON'T STOP GRABBING LIFE WITH BOTH HANDS

Once Christmas was over, all my mates started talking about what they were doing for New Year. And they were pretty much all doing the same thing — heading to Queenstown. I had a bit of a fever on 30 December so I didn't think I'd be going anywhere. The thing with spiking a temperature — especially if you're neutropenic — is that it can be a sign that something else is going wrong. If it got to a certain point I knew I'd have to head straight back to hospital and show them my green card, which would get me past A&E and straight into a ward, where I'd be hooked up to monitors and pumped full of antibiotics. I was monitoring my own temperature, checking it every two hours while I was at home. Thankfully, it didn't spike too high and I got to stay home. That was good. But it wasn't Queenstown.

I knew only two people who *weren't* going to Queenstown. Everyone was there — including Jem — and I'd had accommodation booked for months. I'd been asking the doctors for weeks whether I'd be able to go. They told me that if I flew down, I'd have to go through an airport full of people then sit on a plane with germs potentially circulating in the air. That ruled out flying. They told me that if I drove — Christchurch is about six hours by car from Queenstown — at some stage I'd be three hours from the nearest hospital and if something went really wrong at that point, I'd be at too much risk of dying. That ruled out driving. Actually, it ruled out Queenstown, full-stop. It didn't stop me from asking every doctor and nurse I could to give me some hope that I might make it. Every time the answer was the same: a resounding no.

Come 31 December, I slept until noon, got up, ate and talked to some of my mates, who were — you guessed it — in Queenstown. At 3pm, I was sitting on the couch with my mum — just where every 18-year-old guy wants to be on New Year's Eve at the end of his final year of school. We both had a sense my world was imploding and I could feel my mental stamina cracking. I looked at Mum, and said, 'I want to go to Queenstown.'

I checked out the flights and there was one leaving in 45 minutes, which gave me 15 minutes to get to the airport. I ran into my room, hiffed a whole lot of stuff into a bag and we jumped in the car. Mum sped to the airport, we ran in, and I'd missed check-in. Damn. If only I'd thought about it, I could have checked in online and I would have made my flight.

I was gutted, and, worse than that, I'd told Jem and some of my mates that I was going to try to get there. I'd got their hopes up and now I had to tell them I wasn't coming. I'd got *my* hopes up and now I had to accept that I wasn't going. I felt flatter than I'd been in a long time; I felt absolutely broken.

I told Mum I wanted to be by myself, so I was going for a drive. As I walked out the door, I jokingly said, 'I'll see you when I get back from Queenstown tomorrow.'

She turned around and said, 'Make sure you take your bag. It's got your medication in it.'

Without thinking twice about what I was doing, I grabbed that bag and I walked out the door. I promised Mum I'd update her every hour and agreed that if anything happened to me, she could tell the media that I'd stolen the car. I told her she could also tell them that I left her a beautiful heartfelt note before I left!

I called Jem and told her I was on my way. She said, 'Don't do it!'

As if I wouldn't. I left at 4.30 in the afternoon, knowing that if I drove steadily with a couple of stops I'd make it to Queenstown in time to see in the new year. I called

Dad and told him what I was doing. He didn't believe me at first, and then just told me to take care and have a good time. I also called the hospital, and asked them about my latest blood tests (I didn't tell them where I was!). My neutrophils were around 21, which was one of my highest, and therefore best, results and is about triple the upper end of what a normal person's level would be. I knew I'd be fine.

As promised, I stopped on the hour so I could report in to Mum. The messages went like this:

6pm — 'Just hit Ashburton. Had 750ml of water and two Red Bulls, feeling 100%. Temperature is 37. All good.'
7pm — 'About to hit Fairlie. Nice scenery but bad reception so don't worry if I don't text. Temp is 36.9.'
8pm — 'Just hit Twizel. Temp is 37.1. Past halfway.'
9pm — 'Just got out of Lindis Pass. 37.'

Then I phoned her from Queenstown at about 11.30pm to let her know I'd arrived safely.

I went and found Jem, then we headed into town to watch the fireworks on the waterfront. I caught up with loads of people I hadn't seen in ages. It was the coolest experience. I finally got to sleep at 5am.

After a few hours' sleep, I met up with some mates who were keen for a hair-of-the-dog breakfast, then Jem and I slowly drove back to Christchurch after lunch.

Despite loads of people telling me I shouldn't go,

I reckon that trip did me more good than anything else I'd done in ages. Not going would have been so much worse for me. Emotional well-being plays a huge part in physical well-being. That night was one of the happiest of my life. I was with Jem and my mates, there were fireworks going off, life was *normal* for what felt like the first time in a long while. It gave me the boost I needed to endure the next round of treatment.

The doctors definitely did the right thing in telling me not to go — but really, they'd timed my chemo so that the two days I had off between round three and round four were New Year's Eve and New Year's Day, so what did they expect me to do?

On New Year's Eve, one of the news websites had released their alternative New Year's honours list. They said the aim of the list was to 'take a moment to appreciate a group of people from this great nation and around the world who are making a difference to the lives of the people they touch with our own collection of alternative New Year honourees'.

I didn't find out until a couple of days later that I'd been included on the list. And I was in pretty good company — other honourees included All Black Sonny Bill Williams, New Zealand performer Parris Goebel and actress Emma Watson.

11 | THE END OF CHEMO, HOPEFULLY

When I went back to hospital on 2 January to start what I hoped would be my last round of chemo, a few of the nurses asked me what I'd done for New Year. I told them I'd been for a drive. One asked if I'd watched the fireworks. I replied — quite honestly — that I had (and added 'in Queenstown' in my head!).

That night I went around to a friend's house and, as his parents were away, he decided to have a dinner party. I was pretty impressed — and a little shocked — to see him cook a full dinner of butter chicken from scratch, which was accompanied by a bottle of red wine. To think, just months ago we would have eaten a nasty takeaway with cheap wine straight out of the bottle. It felt very grown-up!

I was back in hospital the next morning for another dose of chemo at 9am, but this time there was no drive-through for me. Round four was six days of R-IVAC chemo — which was more taxing on me and made me throw up more than the R-CODOX — followed by two weeks' rest while the drugs flushed out.

Because I wasn't neutropenic, I was put in a shared room during this stay, which was never fun. There were always people snoring, farting and throwing up. Sleeping wasn't exactly easy in that environment, that's for sure.

THE BEST MEDICAL PROFESSIONALS ENSURE SICK PEOPLE DON'T FEEL LIKE 'JUST ANOTHER CASE'

On a couple of nights when I absolutely had to stay over at the hospital, the nurses were really good to me and let me stay out as late as midnight. I'd sneak in and try not to wake the others in the ward. Unfortunately I did sometimes, but the men who knew they were dying were the most forgiving. They even cheered me on.

There was absolutely no privacy for any of us in the shared room, which I struggled with. So much of your recovery is down to having a positive mindset, and that was pretty hard when three out of the four people in my room were dying.

The guy next to me was having his palliative care organised so they could move him out of the ward. The guy opposite me was told that his cancer was terminal and he had two months to live — the whole room heard it because there was only curtains separating him from me and the two others who were sharing the room. When they pulled back the curtain, his wife fell sobbing onto Mum, who comforted her. It was awful. I thought, 'Right now I should be dealing with new flatmates up in Auckland, not ones in Christchurch Hospital who are in various stages of dying.'

CURVE BALLS CAN COME AT ANY TIME

It was around this time that I started to notice my legs weren't playing ball. I'd sometimes trip over and had rolled my ankles a couple of times.

One day when Jem and I were walking into the hospital, she started teasing me that I was walking like a pukeko. I hadn't noticed until then but she was right. When I walked, my right foot was sticking out at a weird angle. It turned out I had something called peripheral neuropathy — nerve damage caused by the chemotherapy. Or it may have been caused by the damage to my spinal cord from the intrathecal injections.

Nerves are living things and they grow like anything else in your body. Essentially, chemo attacks anything that grows, which is why it kills the cancer, and why your hair falls out. Some chemo patients — including me — find that the treatment also attacks their nerves. I slowly lost the ability to control my legs because the nerves were so damaged they were unable to send their usual signals. The reason my legs were affected first is because the leg nerves are the longest in your body — they go all the way down from your spine to the tips of your toes.

When I was first diagnosed with nerve damage, I was told that it was minor and it was unlikely to get any worse. They were wrong. The control of my big toe went first, then slowly it moved on to my other toes. Then my ankles went and the damage gradually moved further up my legs.

Up until then, everything that could have gone wrong didn't. The blood clot that could have travelled to my heart didn't. The *Staph* infection in my leg that could have got into my heart didn't. The cancer that could have killed me in two weeks if I hadn't been diagnosed didn't. Of course, I was going to be all right. The nerve damage changed that little run of luck.

Damaged nerves caused by chemotherapy are quite a common side-effect of the treatment. I had an extra risk factor that most people don't have to deal with. After they give you intrathecal treatment, they give you folinic acid because it neutralises some of the effects of chemo and stops it from destroying cells. I got given a prescription for folinic acid, which we took to a local pharmacy instead of getting it at the hospital.

The pharmacist made an assumption — somewhat bizarrely — that the doctor had written the wrong thing, so they dispensed folic acid to me. I should have picked it up because I had to take eight tablets of folic acid for a single dose when usually I would take just one of folinic acid. This error wasn't detected until a week later by the hospital pharmacist. Did this have any lasting damage or effect on me? To be honest, we can't be sure. Some doctors have said no, some doctors have said maybe. When we realised what had happened, the pharmacist wrote a letter of apology, but it was a bit scary that I had unneutralised chemo rolling around my body for longer than necessary.

NURSES ARE ABSOLUTE HEROES

I had my last dose of chemo on 6 January. The night before, I'd been over at Jem's eating ice cream and watching Netflix, so I'd got back to hospital at about midnight. I hadn't had a lot of sleep when the nurse gently woke me at 6am. I barely stirred. Then she said, 'I'm just hooking up the bag of chemo now.'

I sat bolt upright with a great fright. In my slumber I had sort of processed what she'd said, but I couldn't understand why she was giving me chemo. Then it slowly dawned on me. She asked me what was wrong and I had to reply, 'Umm, I forgot that I have cancer.' She looked a bit puzzled and carried on with what she was doing. Once I'd worked out what was going on, I rolled back over and slept through my last bag of chemo — hopefully.

Leaving hospital after my chemo was finished was quite strange. My life had revolved around the place for so long that I had come to think of it as my second home. And the thing that made it feel that way was the nurses.

The team of doctors and nurses I worked with, and who saved my life on the BMTU, are the best people I have ever met in my life. They are hardworking, committed, dedicated, but they are caring and considerate, too. This experience would have been a very different one without them by my side, and I consider them all friends. The nurses of the ward became like family to me and it seemed strange that I wouldn't be spending so much time with them anymore.

The relationship that you build with the nurses who work with you is a really unique one, forged in the heat of battle. These people are strangers who are thrust into your world, who see you at your most vulnerable, your worst and your lowest point — a perspective normally reserved for those closest to you, and consequently they become some of the closest people to you. Over time they learn your life story, your hopes, your dreams, your future. And you learn theirs: you ask them how their cat or dog is, what their annoying flatmate has done lately, how the wedding planning is going, or give them a hard time about what school they went to. You spend enough time with each other to have inside jokes, a TV show in common to discuss, a story to share.

They love their work, because, believe me, they have to. There's no other way they would do it. And their love of this work shows through in so many different ways — it brings the ward to life and gives it the energy and hope that stops it from just being a room full of dying people throwing up. They love their patients, and that is what keeps the patients going sometimes, I can tell you from personal experience. It's insanely powerful. They came and talked to me so I didn't just have to stare at the ceiling. They made an effort to get to know my family and me as real people. They hugged me when I cried. They saved my life.

They saw my family and me as part of the team, they listened to my family and me, and considered us in decision-making. They made us feel informed, and as though we had a say and a right to be involved. And it was those things that made them exceptional. I will forever be grateful for what the medical professionals at Christchurch Hospital have done for us, and I will never be able to repay them for that. It was a team of truly incredible people, people who I will forever be connected to, people who saved me, and they did that through collaborating with each other, and with me.

While I was a bit sad not to be seeing the nurses as much anymore, I was pretty happy to say goodbye to some of the guys I had been sharing a room with, and I'm sure the feeling was mutual!

My sense of the hospital changes the more I visit though. While it will always be a positive place for me, it doesn't mean I don't see the pain of others when I go there. Enjoying my visits there can at times feel like a guilty pleasure given

I know what it is like for some of the patients and their families. During a recent visit, I had a great time seeing my old nurses and meeting some new ones, reminiscing a little, and having a real laugh with them.

As I went to leave, I passed the family room. There was a sign on the door saying, 'Do not enter. Meeting in progress.' A glance through the window as I passed showed me a doctor and a nurse sitting opposite a man who had his head in his hands sitting next to a shocked-looking woman. From my time in the ward I knew exactly what was happening, and what it meant for him, for them, for his family. It was a powerful reminder of what this place, which I hold pretty dear to me, really is. Perhaps it was even a shifting point for me — a moment when the BMTU went from a place which was mine, a home to me, to a place in which I must think less of those who went before and more of those who are there now, and how they feel about it. That said, it will always feel like home, and I will always return there.

PEOPLE WITHOUT EYEBROWS LOOK PERMANENTLY SURPRISED

I thought that, once the chemo was done, I would be good to go and things wouldn't get any worse. My hair fell out and I lost a lot of body hair during my treatment, but my eyebrows and my eyelashes didn't fall out until after I'd finished chemo. I thought I'd managed to get through the whole process without losing them. The week after the chemo was done with, however, my eyebrows went, quickly followed by my eyelashes. That really changed the way I looked — it made me appear perpetually surprised. Jem reckoned I looked like Voldemort from *Harry Potter*, which made a change from her saying I looked like Pitbull, the rapper, when my hair fell out!

When my eyelashes started falling out, Jem would count the number I had before I went to sleep, then she'd count them again in the morning to see how many had fallen out overnight. When we got down to single digits, it was pretty sad!

Thankfully, it only took about a month before they started growing back again and I started to look kind of normal. It was another month before my hair started to grow back though. It was faster than I thought it would be, but still not quick enough.

The day after my last dose of chemo, I got the results for the MRI that had been done to try to work out what was going on with my legs. The results came back clear, and Mum started crying. I was a bit confused. I couldn't work it out and then I realised what was going on. 'Ohhh! Did you guys think it was going to be something bad?' It never occurred to me that it could have been a recurrence of the cancer — I just couldn't entertain the idea. The doctor looked at me as if I was a bit of an idiot!

Day 69 (round 4, day 7 of chemotherapy)
Dear Jake

I just have one thing to say about today: when they said your MRI results had come back all clear I sobbed. Wow. Such a massive relief! We (you, Jem, Matt, Harry and I) celebrated with sparkling water in champagne glasses.

You know what I am grateful for today. Amen to that.

I am so proud of you.

Love, your Mum xx

12 | CHOOSING SANITY OVER SAFETY

Jem and I organised a getaway to Akaroa for a night but, before we went, we spent a couple of hours at the mall and had sushi for lunch. What I didn't know at the time was that, even though I felt fine, I was neutropenic. Just being at the mall — never mind eating sushi — could have killed me.

Chemo affects the ability of your bone marrow to produce blood cells so, as well as being neutropenic, my red blood cell count was really low, too. I should have been in hospital in isolation and having a blood transfusion, but instead I was on a romantic getaway. I was feeling so unwell by the time we got back to Christchurch that

I took myself straight to hospital, correctly suspecting I needed a blood and platelet transfusion. I was happy that I was allowed to go home afterwards and didn't have to go back to my bed in the shared ward.

Being neutropenic meant that the tests to discover the amount and cause of the nerve damage in my legs had to be postponed. By this point, I could no longer walk in a straight line or drag my right heel from the knee to the ankle of my left leg while lying down. Whatever was going on, it was clearly getting worse.

A MOTHER IS ONLY AS HAPPY AS HER SADDEST CHILD

The following day, 12 January, I was sitting at home watching TV. I was freezing cold and had a rug over me, and assumed it must have been a chilly day outside. Then Mum walked in wearing shorts and a singlet and said, 'Phew, it's hot in here!' It was 29 degrees outside. We both stared at each other, and I realised I must have had a fever. My temperature was 38.3.

Mum took me straight to A&E. She started crying and saying, 'Please help us! He's got cancer and he's going to pass out!'

Everyone was staring at us. I was unbelievably embarrassed, as I'm sure every teen has been of their parents at some point. I wasn't going to pass out. In fact, I was feeling well enough that I'd refused a wheelchair, which I'd been offered on the way in. Besides which, I had my green card, which I could have given them at the desk and they would have sent me straight over to the BMTU. Seriously, Mum, really?

When I got to the BMTU they put me back into isolation, which, thankfully, meant a room to myself. Numerous blood tests, a chest x-ray and a whole lot of other tests followed. In the meantime they would give me a high dose of antibiotics while the doctors worked out what was wrong with me. The tests showed that it wasn't a bacterial infection so the antibiotics made no difference. I had a virus, and it turned out that Mum and Harry both got a bit sick, too.

My temperature had stabilised seven hours after I'd gone to hospital, but I was still in there four days later, just in case. After having a little bit of my normal life back, being in hospital was unbearable, especially when there was nothing wrong with me, except for the fact that my legs weren't properly working anymore, and there didn't seem to be anything anyone could do about that.

The life that I had finally got a taste of went on without me as I went back to sitting in the same room for days on end. I begged the doctors to discharge me, or even let me out for a day, but to their credit they did the right thing by keeping me in. I knew this was what was best for my safety, but at the same time, 18-year-old guys aren't known for making great decisions around safety.

While I was in hospital my NCEA results arrived. It was a bit strange for me that my mates were all talking about their grades and what it meant for their plans for the year when I had no idea what my year would have in store for me. I got a derived grade pass because I'd been in hospital when the final exams were on. I was lucky that I'd done really well at school during the year so my grades meant that I still qualified to get into university. But to be honest, I wasn't too bothered about them as I had the results of other tests to worry about.

> Take your mock exams at school seriously. If my mocks hadn't been as good as they were, I wouldn't have got University Entrance and I would have had to go back to school to re-do my final year. And to be honest, another year in my calculus class would have been far more likely to kill me than cancer ever was.

It's a wonder they didn't test my speech ability while I was in hospital. Mum reckons having cancer made me mumble. I'm still convinced that it was her hearing at fault. While she was visiting me one day, she was getting all worried that I wasn't letting any of my mates visit me because I was embarrassed by her. She thought I replied, 'You're a shithouse mother.' She didn't react at all and the conversation continued as normal. It wasn't until a bit later that she mentioned it, and I couldn't work out what she was talking about. What I had actually said was, 'I don't give a shit who sees my mother!' It made us both wonder how many similar conversations we'd had over the last few months that hadn't been quite what either of us thought they were.

About that time, Harry was worried that he'd given me cancer. The poor thing thought it was his fault because he'd broken a mercury thermometer at our old house. He thinks a lot for an eight-year-old. Of course, as a typical big brother, I told Mum that she should have told him that it *was* his fault, and that he had to be really nice to me for a long time before I would forgive him!

RULES ARE MADE TO BE BROKEN

After five days in hospital, the doctors said I could go home for a visit one afternoon. I spent a couple of hours hanging out at home with Mum, then she dropped me back at the hospital for my next dose of antibiotics. I decided I wanted to go to Jem's for dinner, and the nurses said that would be fine so long as I was back at 11pm for my next round of pills. Yeah, right.

I packed my bag and texted Jem to ask her to pick me up. We went back to her place and I told her I wasn't going back to hospital that night. She looked a bit worried but she knew I wasn't joking. At midnight, with a strange mix of smugness and fear, I dialled the number for the BMTU to let them know I wouldn't be back. The nurse who answered the phone was one of the ones I was a little bit scared of. Shit. I knew I was probably in for an earful so I quickly said, 'Hiit'sJakeBaileyhere.

I'mnotcomingbacktonight.I'llbebacktomorrow. OKBYE.'
And hung up without giving her a chance to reply.

The next morning I turned up with a little trepidation, but faced no consequences. I think it might have been something they suspected would happen, especially with an 18-year-old patient on their hands. Ironically, I was discharged that day anyway. It was another case of the doctors doing the right thing and taking care of me, but me needing to just get out and live my life a little bit. Sometimes I had to choose my sanity over my safety.

Day 78 (round 4, day 16 of chemotherapy)
Dear Jake

Today you got out of hospital for the first time since Tuesday. A rainy day and we watched a bit of telly before you went back to get some antibiotics and headed to Jem's for tea. Now I'm waiting to see if you return home to be taken into the hospital by 12am or if you are going to flag it for tonight. I know you aren't keen to return and you ran it past the nurses and didn't get a terrible reaction.

I felt for you when we were driving into the hospital and you touched briefly on how hard the last few months have been. Thank you for thanking me for giving you freedom when you are out of hospital (to take off to Queenstown, Timaru etc).

It has been conflicting for me at times but, as I said to that woman from CanTeen, that's for me to process. Nearly losing you has been gut-wrenching for me, a pain I couldn't have grasped fully before it happened. But now you have a second shot at life and it is so important you make the most of it. Of course I'd like to keep you close and wrap you in cotton wool, but I know the best thing is to let you embrace life even more than you would have before cancer. Ironically, the old saying 'suck the marrow out of life' comes to mind.

I am grateful for:
1. You.
2. The depth of the conversations we have as well as our light-hearted banter.
3. The hours cancer has given us to be together, hanging, watching TV, talking, listening, joking, but not crying because I am not allowed to do that.
4. The generosity of your spirit — I notice it daily.
5. Your thoughtfulness. I was taken aback when you thanked me.

I love you, Jake. You really are outstanding.
Love, Mum x

NOT EVERY PERSON WHO STUMBLES IS DRUNK

The night I was discharged, I took Jem out to dinner to a lovely little Japanese restaurant. The place had a huge glass frontage that opened out onto the carpark. My legs were pretty bad by that point, but I wasn't using crutches yet. Getting into the restaurant was fine as I leaned on Jem as we walked in.

After dinner was a different story, though. As I made my way out to the car I was stumbling all over the place as if I was really drunk — I wasn't — and managed to crash into a couple of other tables along the way. There were a few people giving me sideways glances. Then I staggered my way around to where my car was parked while everyone sat there watching me. I got into the car and switched the lights on, which proceeded to light up the whole restaurant, and then drove away. Fortunately, at that stage my legs still allowed me to drive normally. I felt so awkward, but I'm kind of relieved yet slightly freaked out that no one said or did anything after seeing what looked like a very drunk guy get into his car.

Unsurprisingly, it was back to hospital the next day, but thankfully as an outpatient. My platelets were really low, as were my neutrophils and haemoglobin. None of that was particularly surprising, but I would have liked better results in what was hopefully my last week of chemo.

DON'T ADOPT ALL THE SUGGESTIONS YOU READ IN BOOKS ON CANCER

Mum's email a couple of days before the end of my last round of chemotherapy had me in fits:

Dear Jake

Today I read a book about the mother of a 17-year-old with cancer. She made cards with 'Jeff is happy, healthy and healed' and gave them to all his friends. See, there are some mothers out there more embarrassing than me. I've made some for your friends anyway . . .

Jake is hairless (well almost), humorous (not referring to when he walks) and hungry (due to his mother's poor cooking skills — please feed).

NOT ALL RADIATION IS BAD

That Friday I had a PET scan as a final check that the cancer was gone. It officially marked the end of cycle four and, hopefully, the end of chemo altogether. In the scan, they inject you with radioactive glucose that then goes to wherever anything is growing, like tumours. After they'd injected it into me, I was apparently emitting the same amount of radiation as Chernobyl from 150 metres away. That meant that the procedure had to be done in a lead-lined room. The person who administers the injection does it and then gets the hell out of there. Then I walked to the PET scanner while everyone else keeps their distance. Everyone has their own personal Geiger counters so they could measure the amount of radiation that they were being exposed to.

One of the haematologists who was working with me reckoned that I'd had about 30 years' worth of radiation, if you included the four CT scans and two PET scans I'd had. That was slightly alarming. Mind you, it's not like I was worried about it giving me cancer!

My main haematologist, who had given me my diagnosis all those months ago, phoned me that afternoon with the preliminary results. There was no indication of cancer in my body. But they still wanted to check out a glow in my bone marrow. She said they were pretty sure it was just caused by the bone marrow regenerating, but they wanted to be more certain before they could confirm that I was in remission.

And with that, after 83 days, the chemotherapy was over. Because of all the radiation I was emitting I went home to Dad's as I wasn't allowed to be around anyone under the age of 15, and I couldn't be around animals, so Mum's place with Harry and the cat was out of the question.

13 | LET'S TALK ABOUT CANCER

About a month or so later, I went to have lunch with a bunch of friends. While we were eating, one of my mates said to me, 'Oh, this'll be the first time you've been back to Velvet Burger since . . . ahhh . . . ahhh . . . since . . .'

I jumped in with, 'Do you mean, since I got cancer?'

He said, 'Yeah, since that . . .'

I think he was a bit worried that mentioning it might upset me, but it's not like I hadn't noticed that I'd had cancer! Or as if I'd forgotten about it and he'd just reminded me.

It's one thing when someone who knows I've had cancer doesn't want to talk about it. It's a whole different story when people who don't know about it ask a lot of questions then don't like the answers.

Usually when people I don't know asked me about being on crutches or the scar under my eye, I'd just say, 'It's a long story.' If they pushed it, I'd say, 'It's a long story that involves cancer.' I liked it when people would just take that in their stride. If they got uncomfortable, I'd just think, 'Well, you asked.'

I have a scar of sorts, a dark mark under one eye, by my cheek bone, caused because a tumour grew under it, and as it shrunk, the skin scarred and darkened. I was sitting in a café one day and the owner came up to me and motioned towards my eye and said, 'Did you get that in a fight?' I smiled, and said, 'No'. 'Did you fall down the stairs?' I smiled again. 'No.' She wasn't going to let this one go. 'Oh well, what have you done to yourself?' There was nothing for it. 'I got cancer.' She almost passed out, and her apologies wouldn't stop. Let's just say I got a free coffee out of it!

> Embrace your scars. I have been asked whether physical post-cancer scars bother me (few as they are). Maybe it comes from the intense focus my generation has on how we look. The truth is, I know of lots of people who had body parts removed because of cancer and were left with much worse scars than mine. I try not to think of it as 'another thing cancer has done to me', but as the closest thing I will ever get to the military

> medals my great-grandparents and grandparents
> got pinned on their chests, and I treasure mine.

Another time, the barista at a café near the hospital in Christchurch pointed at my PICC line and said, 'What have you done to your arm?' The fact that I was wearing a beanie despite it being 30 degrees outside should have tipped him off, or maybe the fact I had no eyebrows . . . but, no. I just blurted out, 'I got cancer.' It wasn't malicious at all, but the guy recoiled like I had punched him, and the mouths of everyone there just dropped open.

My complete disregard for the social stigmas around cancer has got me into hot water a few times now. But the thing is, for me, cancer isn't uncomfortable or shocking. Cancer is a part of my past, my history, what makes up the story of my life. I'm not afraid of it or uncomfortable talking about it, and I reckon it would help a lot of other people get through it if everyone else would talk about it, too.

It's amazing the number of people who are so uncomfortable with the concept of cancer that they can't even say the word. There's a lot of taboo around cancer — some people even call it 'the big C'. It's stupid.

Everyone hates talking about it, yet everyone knows someone who has died from it. I know it makes people uncomfortable, but I think people need to talk about it more and make it less scary. It's not as frightening as it used to be — having cancer no longer means a death sentence.

Part of my issue with the stigma around talking about

cancer is that that stigma can be transferred onto the patients. This can sometimes be the worst part about having cancer — you've got something wrong with you and you kind of want to feel sorry for yourself, but for some reason you end up feeling guilty for having it because it makes people so uncomfortable.

I always took the view that it was me who had it, not them, and it wasn't like they could catch it. I couldn't understand why they'd feel uncomfortable. I would have preferred it if they could have just had a laugh with me about it and make the whole situation easier on both of us.

It shouldn't have been my responsibility to make anyone else feel comfortable about me having cancer.

> It's hard to know what to say to someone who is sick. Here's what not to say. Don't say sorry. It's not your fault. So many people told me they were sorry, and I'd think 'Why are you sorry? Did you give me cancer?'
>
> Remember that when people say dumb things, it's because they don't know what to say.

14 | LIFE IN LIMBO

While the chemotherapy had ended, day one of what Mum came to call 'limbo' had begun. That limbo period only lasted until all my tests were completed and the results were back, but we didn't really know how long that would take.

On day four of 'limbo', 26 January, I went into the Children's Haematology and Oncology Centre — or CHOC for short — to have another bone marrow aspiration done. Before the procedure I met with one of the haematologists who reckoned that the results of the tests they'd already done looked so good they almost didn't bother with the bone marrow — but that they'd decided to do it, just to be on the safe side.

I also learned that my main haematologist had been

speaking to an American colleague, who was one of the world-leading experts on Burkitt's. He'd confirmed that he thought four rounds of chemo would be all I'd need, and he also didn't think I'd need a stem cell transplant. This was all good news. I felt particularly reassured to hear that an expert believed I'd received the best treatment programme possible.

The other thing the haematologist did was start the ball rolling on an application to ACC (Accident Compensation Commission) for the cost of the physiotherapy I needed on my legs. It was a good thing he did, as it took about five months for the application to be approved, and it was becoming pretty clear I was going to need as much help as I could get.

I was given a general anaesthetic to have the bone marrow test done. Since it was — hopefully — my last one, I asked the doctor to take some pics of me when I was knocked out, for posterity. I later checked my phone to find some selfies of the surgical team, with me unconscious in the background!

When I woke up from the anaesthetic, I was still very out of it. I rolled over and thought that the nurse who was sitting with me was Jem. The first thing I said to her was 'I love you.' Great start. I don't think the feeling was mutual.

At the same time, another nurse was talking to a patient on the other side of the room. I thought she was talking to me so I kept shouting out to her. She'd say, 'Are you okay? Do you want a drink?' to this other guy. And I'd roar across at her, 'Nah, I'm all right, thanks!' Eventually she turned around and said, 'I'm not talking to you!'

In the adult ward, where I'd spent most of my time, it was all very clinical and organised. In the kids' ward — where people up to the age of 16 go — it was like going into a pre-school. They had little couches, and little pumps for their medicine, and teddy bears everywhere. I was sitting on this bright-pink couch waiting for my appointment, and I had the most surreal experience.

Some kids were playing around me. I looked up and there were these little thin, bald kids running around chasing each other, giggling. I sat there thinking, had it not been for the fact they were bald, I wouldn't have guessed that this wasn't just a normal pre-school. The kids were so happy.

I guess that's the power of the spirit of children, and their ability to influence their surroundings — it didn't matter why they were there, or what they all had in common to bring them together. Nor what lay ahead of them, or what they had been through. When they were put together, they were all just kids, and they absolutely lit the place up.

It was hard to believe that they had cancer, except for their bald heads and the bunch of really tired, worried-looking parents sitting around the outside of the room. The kids were having a great time. They were completely oblivious to how bad or sad their situation might have been. It was so surprising and so beautiful at the same time. I almost felt like I was part of their family because

I was just another bald kid in there with them. I was part of a pretty special, unique club at that moment. But at the same time, I didn't really identify with them in that way, because I didn't see myself as a cancer patient. I was thinking 'These poor little kids' when actually I was one of them.

The day after my last test to check that the cancer was all gone, my allowance from the government for my headwear arrived. The budget is set so that people who lose their hair through chemo can buy wigs. I had no intention of buying a wig. I joked about buying a merkin (Google it!) but all I really needed were a couple of beanies — and I'd been sent heaps of those from all over the world. Nevertheless, I was determined to spend that money on covering my head in the most extravagant way I could think of. I looked for beanies by Gucci, Armani and Louis Vuitton but such things apparently don't exist. So I settled on a $215 Ralph Lauren beanie!

I was quite surprised to find the media interest in me continued right throughout my treatment. As a result, the school organised a PR company to take over as the media contact for me. While I was having the tests at the end of my chemo, I knew there was a risk that my status would be leaked to the media. The PR company suggested I write a media release, which could be sent out as soon as I had my results through. It seemed like a good idea, although it felt really strange to be writing a statement saying that I was in remission when I didn't actually know if I was.

REMISSION DOESN'T MEAN A RETURN TO HOW THINGS WERE

On 29 January, three months after I'd gone into hospital, I had one of my regular appointments with my haematologist. It was a Thursday, and she told me that my bone marrow biopsy fluid was clear of cancer but they were waiting on the results of a core biopsy. She said the results would probably come in early the following week.

A few hours later, I was sitting in bed and Mum came into my room sobbing. I thought, 'Here we go!'

I really thought she was coming with bad news. She flopped onto the bed, and sobbed, 'You're in remission!'

And with that, another passage in my life drew to a close. Cheers for an interesting few months, cancer, but it will take a hell of a lot more than that to take me out.

While Mum cried tears of relief and happiness, I didn't feel a single thing. Not relief, not happiness, not empowerment or courage, or any of that stuff that is associated with anyone lucky enough to have survived what I just had. It was like running a marathon but, instead of finishing it with the big grin when you cross the line, you opt to keep running on, away from the cheering crowd and happy people, back to your car, and drive home to sit alone and contemplate what had been achieved.

We managed to tell my family and my close friends about it before the media release went out. I texted Nic Hill from CBHS and told him that he could put a statement up on the school's website.

In the media statement, I got to fulfil a promise I'd made to my BMTU nurse, Georgia. We used to joke that she was the only reason I'd done the speech — and it is true, she was. She would laugh, and then tell me that once I got famous I'd have to tell everyone that. In my remission interviews, I talked about her and made sure I thanked her for making sure I got there that night.

The full statement

For the last three months, I have undertaken intensive chemotherapy for Burkitt's non-Hodgkin's lymphoma.

In response to the incredible and at times overwhelming interest and support in my battle with cancer, I am now fortunate to be able to announce that recent tests show that my treatment has been successful and I am officially in remission.

There will be a lot of follow-up care over the coming years, and cancer makes no guarantees, but for now I can get on with my life.

There is a massive team of people I want to thank:

Firstly, my family and friends, who have been on this long, rough journey with me. I could not have got through it without the people who have been by my side.

My medical team from the Bone Marrow Transplant Unit at Christchurch Hospital. You saved my life. I am in great admiration and debt of your caring, with over-whelming respect for not only what you do, but how you do it.

The Christchurch Boys' High family for the amazing

support they have given me. The benefit of such a tight-knit brotherhood has been so evident.

To the public for their heartfelt messages, which have been exceptionally uplifting. I was blown away by what an impact my words had on strangers, and then I was blown away by what an impact strangers' words had on me. Some of the letters I received were incredibly humbling.

I'd like to make special mention of the blood and platelet donors whose donations helped save my life. To the nurse who encouraged me to get out of my hospital bed and deliver my final speech at prizegiving. To the ward cleaner whose smiles always made a difference to my mornings. Thank you.

Finally, I also want to mention the media, who don't always have a good reputation, but in my case have been extremely respectful to my family and me.

I also want to acknowledge the other people who are undergoing treatment for cancer who have not necessarily received the same amount of support that I have. I wish them and their families the best. I hope, like us, you experience moments of genuine depth amongst your hardship — moments probably missed if we didn't have to go through this.

The thing about facing death is that you get to rethink exactly who you are and who you want to be if you are lucky enough to live through it. I want to make a difference more than ever before. Our lives are simply too fleeting not to.

So, during this gap year before I go to university,

I would like to use my experiences to help young people or others who are facing challenges by telling my story in schools or other audiences. Perhaps I might be able to motivate or help others deal with their own struggles.

The chemotherapy has taken a huge toll on my body. It has left me with ongoing issues and it will take me time to get back to where I was previously. Sometimes I feel more like 81 than 18.

But I'm just grateful to be alive.

Jake Bailey

About 20 minutes after the statement was sent out, I was sitting there checking the messages on my phone and I got a breaking news notification from one of the news apps. It said: 'Inspirational school boy Jake Bailey's cancer in remission.' What the hell? It seemed so weird that the interest in me was that great that it was breaking news.

I felt like I was in the middle of a hurricane. Everyone around me was celebrating, everyone was talking about me, but I sat in my room for most of it. I don't know what was going on in my head, maybe it was emotional numbness, but I was not in the place that I thought I would be and I found that really disconcerting. Jem wasn't there at the time and she's still quite upset that she couldn't be there for me. I spent a lot of time talking to her on the phone that night.

I was trending on social media as people celebrated my 'wellness', my family were drinking champagne and partying, and I was in bed, feeling no real emotion about the news, talking to Jem and laughing at some of the negative comments about me on social media. It's amazing how nasty some people can be without realising or caring that the people they're aiming at might see what they're saying. I was feeling pretty flat at the time but I knew that, however odd I was feeling, my life wasn't as tragic as those people's.

Day 90 (the day you were officially told you are in remission)
Dear Jake

Where do I begin? I can barely think how to write this . . .

Today we went to outpatients to get your dressing changed and were told that the bone marrow biopsy fluid was clear, and that they were just waiting on the core.

I got a phone call around 5.30, which I took in the laundry to get away from The Bee Gees' music. I cried so much that the doctor apologised, but I told him it was a good thing I was crying. A photo was taken by your photographer (oh that would be me) and the statement and photo released. I rang Steve, who sobbed like me/with me. Then I sent 61 texts and made four phone calls in my ensuite so I could cry some more. Before Steve, Katrina and your dad could get here, you were in the *Herald*, on the Stuff news website and on the TV1 news page. It seems you were even on TV3 news but we missed it.

Three bottles of expensive Champagne sat on the table for the first time ever (along with a bottle of whiskey). We toasted you and talked about the last three months (to the day — which is a little spooky). Steve kept grounding you for getting cancer. Harry wanted to know if he can use the toilet in what has become your bathroom again now.

Phew! You are so loved. And again you are taking off into stardom with people interested in having you come and give a motivational speech already! What a way to launch a career!

One massive big thank you today (which I could repeat five times, but . . .)

I'm so very grateful Jake is in remission! You bloody legend.

So much love and admiration for you, Jake. Mum xx

REMISSION JUST MEANS NO CANCER
AT THE MOMENT

As soon as my remission was announced, I had requests to do speaking engagements. It was hard to explain to some people that just because I was in remission it didn't mean that I was back to my normal healthy self. I'd only recently finished chemotherapy, and just because I didn't have cancer anymore it didn't mean I was well enough to be doing anything much. A lot of people seemed to think that being in remission is the same as being cured and back to how I was before. It's not. All it means is that the cancer has gone away — there's still a hell of a lot of healing that needs to take place before life goes anywhere near back to normal.

> If you're going through chemotherapy, try to think beyond it and plan for what happens when it's finished. That way, you won't find yourself thinking, 'What happens now?' For many — if not all — cancer survivors, remission is the mid-point rather than the end of the journey.

It turned out my thanking the media for being so respectful was a little bit premature. While I was having treatment they were great, but once I was in remission it felt a bit like it was open season on me. There were reporters threatening to doorstep our house until I spoke to them, there were reporters calling, trying to trick Mum into talking to them — the gloves were off.

Later that week, I spent a morning doing a whole bunch of interviews. But that seemed to just make people want to know more. In order to handle all the media requests in one go, I set aside a whole day about a week later. I hoped that would make them leave me alone for a little while. I did two international interviews — *The Times* and *The Daily Mail* — over the phone, a live one with Mike Hosking, and then I talked with *3 News*, *Seven Sharp*, *One News*, *The Press*, *The Star*, *The New Zealand Herald*, *Woman's Day* . . . you name it. I basically sat in the same room all day but changed my clothes every now and then so the interviews didn't all look the same. Each interviewer had 30 minutes to ask whatever they wanted and take whatever photos they needed. As a result, I was back on televisions and front pages all over the country.

In between, I was back at the hospital having more tests. This time they weren't for cancer but to try to get to the bottom of my nerve damage. I was meant to have some more intrathecal treatments but my haematologist decided that the risk of more nerve damage was greater than the risk of the cancer returning. Effectively, I never completed the full treatment regime they had planned for me.

THERE'S ALWAYS SOMETHING TO BE GRATEFUL FOR

Day 102 (day 12 of remission)
Dear Jake

Today you bought some clothes, and I returned some clothes on your request, and I bought some clothes. Today I looked at some pretty cute video recordings of you as a little fella.

Today I said we all have to do things we don't like and I mentioned going to the hospital when you had cancer and watching Mum die. I'd like to correct what I said because I didn't quite express what I meant. I meant that I really, really didn't enjoy watching you and Mum suffer. Those were two of the hardest things I've ever endured. Still, I suppose if I did enjoy those things you might have had grave concerns for my mental well-being.

I actually didn't mind going to hospital to see you. There were things I was grateful for every time I went. Here's some of them:
1. Firstly, that I wasn't going to the morgue to see you. Or that bloody hospital viewing room, where I have seen two dead loved ones.
2. Everyone washed their hands before they entered and umpteen times in between.
3. You and I got to spend heaps of time together. Time we would not have had if you were not sick. Time that made me feel closer to you. Time to just chat. Or just sit and be.
4. The nurses and doctors were great. And fun. And one of them was sexy.

5. You had some interesting visitors (and stalkers) and fan mail. That stuff was better than what was on TV. Oh, and you had TV as well.
6. It was an escape from the busy world outside. Time to contemplate life and other such stuff. Almost like a meditative place.
7. Each day I suspected was a day closer to your discharge and announcement of remission.
8. We had some pretty good laughs in amongst the rubble.
9. There was access to free cups of tea.
10. The cooking made my cooking look good. Even though you joked that my cooking gave you cancer.
11. I would text lots of people while I was sitting there. All of those relationships were strengthened too.
12. There was always someone worse off and it made me feel that we were lucky.
13. And, unlike you, I was able to leave. I would step outside and gulp the fresh air and feel guilty. And sad for you. I'd say a prayer for you. And go home and write to you.

We love you, Jake. We want to support you the best we can to get through the next stage of this. Just tell us what you need from us, and also what you don't need.

Love, Mum x

15 | THANK YOU, CANCER

In some ways, remission was a hell of a lot harder than having cancer. Being told that I didn't have cancer was almost more difficult than being told I did have cancer. I didn't feel happy or excited or anything. I had lost my protective cocoon of the hospital. I had been so focused on beating the cancer that, once it was gone, I sat there thinking, 'What do I do now?'

The answer to that question was 'make my legs work again'. The nerve damage caused by the chemo was so bad I couldn't walk. Actually, it was so bad I was told I might never walk again. Okay, so I'd beaten cancer but it felt like my life had still been ruined.

> If you're going to be there to support someone through cancer, it's perhaps more important that you do it after the treatment and when they're in remission, rather than when everyone is there for them during their treatment.

YOU DON'T REALISE HOW MUCH YOU USE YOUR LEGS UNTIL YOU CAN'T CONTROL THEM

I couldn't roll over in bed because I couldn't move my legs. I needed to be carried up and down stairs. I was on two crutches, dragging myself around, so nothing felt like it had gone back to normal.

I think I handled the nerve damage a lot worse than I handled having cancer. As well as the control, I lost quite a bit of the feeling in my feet and lower legs. I'd try to move my legs in a specific way and they'd move, but not in the way I was telling them to. If I lifted my leg straight up in the air, it would go all over the place. The messages just weren't getting through from my brain.

I underwent a heap of tests to assess just how much damage there was. As well as sending electric pulses down my legs, I had to try to do a whole lot of things. Could I walk on my heels for a distance? Could I walk on tippy toes for a distance? The damage had been gradually getting worse throughout January. Eventually, I went from not being able to walk steadily, to not being able to walk without someone near me, to not being able to walk without having someone to cling onto.

When I stayed at Jem's place overnight, to go to the toilet I'd get out of bed then crawl on my hands and knees from the bed to her desk, then I'd shimmy along the desk to the wall, then I'd hold onto the wall across to the door of the ensuite. Once I was in the bathroom, I'd hold onto the shower door to get across to the toilet. Once I'd been to the toilet, I had to repeat the whole process in reverse to get back to bed.

That was the worst time of my life, easily. The hardest part was that, even though I was being told the nerves would probably regenerate, I never knew for certain. The doctors kept saying, 'It might come back, but we can't be sure of that. Be prepared for the possibility that it might not come back and the fact that you might not walk again.' That made everything worse.

I couldn't ever have imagined life going on like that. I honestly don't know what I would have done. At my darkest moments, I wondered if I would have wanted to live. My life felt completely destroyed. It gave me a whole new level of admiration for people who are in wheelchairs, because I don't know if I would have been strong enough to live like that. It seemed a bit unfair to have beaten cancer but still have my life ruined.

I lost the ability to do basic things. That made me really angry. Mum would have to carry everything for me. I couldn't go out on my own because I couldn't walk more than 100 metres, even very slowly. This seemed to affect my life more than cancer or chemo did. When

I had cancer and was having treatment, I still felt pretty independent, even though I was in hospital most of the time. Not being able to walk took that independence away from me and I hated it.

I'd be at Jem's place and I'd be hungry, but I wouldn't want to ask anyone to get me food. The kitchen was downstairs and I didn't want to go down there because I would quite often fall down the steps. So I just wouldn't eat. Jem didn't mind helping me but I hated feeling so dependent.

I began collapsing randomly. In the shower one morning, I fell and hit my head. Outside, I took chunks out of my knees every time I went down and, because my immunity was low, I didn't heal very quickly or cleanly.

YOU CAN BE WEAK BY FATE, BUT STRONG IN WILL

That feeling of uselessness sometimes transformed into something a little more scary. One day, at Jem's, I wanted a cup of tea and couldn't go and make one. For a split second, the thought flew through my head, 'If I had died, I wouldn't have to deal with this. If I'd died, this wouldn't be a problem.'

After that happened, I felt really terrible. I felt like I was almost wishing that I'd died and I wasn't grateful for being spared. It was dark and quite scary. Eventually, I talked to other cancer survivors about it, and most of them had experienced similar things at different points.

That made me feel a little bit better about it.

Looking back, I think it happened because my brain was coming to terms with the fact that I didn't die after coming so close. I think it was also a reaction to having a new normal, a new life I found myself in. I had to adjust to these imposed changes and to the fact I couldn't just step back into my old life, the one I was loving before I got cancer.

It was tough going out in public. I felt more conspicuous because of the nerve damage than I ever did when I had chemo. I was just like Timmy in *South Park*, the way I dragged my legs around on crutches. I was always terrified I'd fall over in public, too, as my balance was badly affected. I didn't realise that balance is dictated not only by your inner ear, but also by the sensation of pressure on your feet. I couldn't feel that normal pressure so I was at a far greater risk of falling over. The combination of no sensation in my feet with the inability to tell my legs what to do meant that I never knew if I was going to fall over until I was just about to hit the ground. Doing that in public would have been embarrassing. Being a normal teenage guy who hates doing anything dumb in public was compounded by the fact that people knew who I was.

In these bleak times I learnt some lessons about the ability of courage to keep me from dark places. Nevertheless, the hardest thing to work through was that both the dark place and the courage resided in my head.

ALWAYS HAVE SOMETHING TO LOOK FORWARD TO

On top of dealing with my legs not working, I had to face up to the fact that Jem was soon going to be moving to another country. On 17 February, three days after Valentine's Day and three weeks after the announcement of my remission, Jem was on a plane bound for university on the Gold Coast. We both hated being separated, but we knew it was for the best. That didn't make it any easier though. Saying goodbye was horrible.

By late February, I was as flat as can be — it was awful. All my mates had gone to university, and most of them were in other cities. My plan to study commerce and law in Auckland had long since gone out the window. I couldn't go back to work because of my nerve damage, and I had loved working at that bar. My girlfriend had moved to another country and I didn't know when I was going to see her next. I had no eyebrows, eyelashes or hair, and my legs didn't work. I just felt completely left behind while everyone else was off making new lives for themselves.

The plan was that eventually I'd move to Australia to be with Jem, but I couldn't even think about going until my legs were better. It made me so angry — I'd look at them and think 'Just fucking get better!' I don't think that helped.

At my lowest point, two days after Jem had left, Mum booked us a trip to the Gold Coast. It really gave me something to look forward to, but I was a bit worried about how expensive it was. Mum laughed it off, saying it was easier than having to give me a bit of her liver or a kidney or something!

For the two weeks before we headed to Australia, I worked really hard at physio to try to force my legs to get better. That really took it out of me.

I was still getting a lot of mail from overseas at the time, including letters from an English class in Morocco. That was pretty amazing and kept my spirits up!

But the moment of joy that gave me was cut short when I opened the next letter, which was one of several I received from so-called Christians warning me that I was going to hell when I died (which they seemed to believe was imminent) unless I repented immediately. It's pretty hard to understand what's going through the minds of people who send stuff like that.

I remember Mum and I had a great talk about my cancer at this time. She told me that she would now go out of her way to drive around the hospital instead of driving past it because it made her heart race. I was quite surprised, as I was — and am — always happy to call in there to see the nurses. I go back to the hospital, the place where I had the worst time of my life, because it holds so many memories of good times I had with the staff there, many more than the bad ones. It made me realise that neither of us will ever understand the other person's experience of my cancer. For me, in many ways, it had such a positive effect on my life that I'm quite grateful for it, whereas for Mum it was the worst time in her life and she absolutely hated it.

> Once you are in remission, people might begin sharing how things were for them. Some of this can be hard to hear. It can also help everyone process what happened if you are able to discuss it together.

My brother Harry wrote a poem about how it had been for him. It goes:

Mirror

My life is a mirror
and my brother's cancer is a hammer
that smashes against my mirror.
I can't stop the pieces falling out.
Sometimes I stick them back into place
but they just fall out again.

As powerful as it is, this is pretty hard for me to read. My brother's hurt hurts me. I even feel some guilt about how his life changed when I was sick and all the worry he experienced. I do, however, respect his need to process what happened for him and, when the poem got published in the kids' journal *Toitoi*, I was immensely proud of the little guy and relieved that something positive had come out of this time for him.

When I was in hospital, my little sister Scarlett would draw pictures for me — showing us together before I got sick. Those pictures were great motivation for me to get back to those happy times. It did make me wonder how hard it was for her not having her big brother around.

Mum also wrote a bit about her experience of my illness. It's hard for me to read it as I still hate thinking about what everyone has been through, but here are some extracts from it:

Our celebrations that Jake is in remission have been tempered with respect towards the people who have lost a child or loved one to cancer and to those in battle. It is almost unbelievable that we lost my mother Elaine to cancer the year before Jake was diagnosed. There was none in our family and then it was like we were taking pesticides in our tea instead of milk.

I knew on the day we were told it was cancer my family would never be the same. It's been an intensive period of self-discovery and growth whether we wanted to grow or not. None of us are the same person we were when we stumbled into this. Adversity builds character. I've learnt about mindfulness — to stay in the now. I've learnt about facing fear, acceptance and patience. I have more to learn about forgiveness and self-acceptance.

I no longer have any control over my family's destiny. In truth, I never had, but it was a nice illusion. This was bigger than me and I had to surrender to the process. I handed my boy over to the medical professionals. My 18-year-old son — still at school and living under my roof — was making adult decisions, like whether or not he would consent to treatment. At times we were asked to leave the room so he could be spoken to in private. I worried whether he had all he needed as he was thrust to a point beyond that when a lad transitions into a man. Cancer defined the stage when I let my son go and watched him become a man confronting his own mortality.

Jake has taken it in his stride. He has lived the values he spoke of in his speech and they have carried him a long way. He stuck to them in the toughest of times. He overtook me in intellect and character from an early age. Probably about the time he got out of nappies. At that point all I had on him was that I could drive and he couldn't — simply because he couldn't reach the pedals. I remember a five-year-old Jake imparting wisdom. One day, when he was five years old, I asked him what he had so far learnt about life. We turned his answer into a piece of art, capturing mature insight next to little handprints. He said:

'Love and care for others; be patient; help others when they need you; don't push in line; thank God; be kind; don't try and make yourself look like someone else or be like someone else when they are better than you because you are good and friendly how you are; eat good food and treats but not all the time because some countries don't have food; care about others; don't hurt people; have fun with your friends, run with them, play with them, when they are hurt give them a sticking plaster; do chores; be responsible; smile at people when they look miserable or lost; always be happy or do something if you are not; make good choices and think about other people's feelings. Yes, I think that is about it.'

I feel the guilt only a mother whose child is diagnosed with stage four cancer knows. I turned the energy I could have spent wrestling that monster into being there for my boys. Connection mattered. I couldn't be at the hospital all the time and when I was, I wasn't with Harry. I had to find ways of being where I wasn't. For Jake it became a daily email before my bed each night. Most were sent between 12 and 2am, when I got to finally sit down and pause in the quiet. A few arrived closer to 4am. They've probably meant more to me than him. For Harry it was a note in his lunchbox with a chocolate attached. One day I saw him open it from afar. Three kids were sitting around him. He read the message aloud and popped the chocolate in his mouth while they looked on longingly. After Jake was diagnosed, Harry moved into the master bedroom for a while. He would wake at 3am and, while we assured him it was going to be okay, he would ask questions that couldn't be answered. 'Is Jake going to die?' 'When is Jake coming home?' 'When can we have our old life back?' 'Will I get cancer?' 'Will you guys get cancer?' 'Is the cat going to die?' 'When are you going to die, Mum and Dad?'

Before they passed away, my parents, Malcolm and Elaine, had been there for Jake and me every step of our way. Right from the beginning, when my father enthusiastically dragged my mother to the maternity hospital when they heard I was going into labour. As I staggered out of the lift during a contraction I was greeted by their smiley faces — my father holding out a bunch of flowers. Their absence has felt more enormous than ever recently.

Over this time I listened to what people had to say. I concluded that the world is made up of those who have faced crushing hardship/trauma/loss or their own mortality, and those who have not. Of those who have, some have grown from it and turned their experiences into lessons worth hearing. I would incorporate their wisdom into my framework. My brother Steve (who conquered meningitis as a teen and conquers mountains for fun) offered Winston Churchill-esque words that spurred me forward. He made it his job to support me so I could support Jake and on one of our several midnight phone calls he convinced me I shouldn't view this as yet another family tragedy, but see Elaine's cancer as our training ground. We were consequently better placed to help Jake survive. During another call when Jake's kidneys were failing, he reassured me we would do 'whatever it takes' to get through. This became my mantra. I hung onto words like these at the hardest of times. I stuck words next to my bed so they were there when I opened my eyes in the morning. I played songs with meaningful lyrics that helped me climb out of bed when I would have preferred to pull the covers over my head and hide from my fear of Jake's death.

I wasn't me when Jake had cancer. Well, of course I was me, but I wasn't the person I wanted to be, and at times even someone I recognised. I did things I never do. A hospital secretary admitted they had lost his MRI referral and said they would ring me with a triage appointment immediately. Hours later, when the call hadn't come I went to the hospital and spoke loudly (okay… perhaps shouted) at some poor employee who ironically stood in front of a sign stating "Verbal abuse will not be tolerated in this hospital". When I caught myself, I apologised profusely and said "I know it's not your fault but…" and started off again. I don't take tablets on a daily basis but I took about 1400 tablets from the herbalist. Tablets to keep me well, to help me sleep, vitamins. Drops to calm me when I was anxious. The drops to stimulate my appetite tasted so bad they made me too nauseous to eat. I watched *American Horror Story* while writing to Jake at night and found it less scary than my real life. Despite a passionate dislike of running I found it easy because my adrenaline was pumping. I divided the kilometres into quarters and each represented a round of Jake's chemo. If I got tired or wanted to stop I'd reflect on how Jake couldn't and how much easier it was to run than have cancer. I felt jealous and angry at supermarket-strangers who were grumbling at 'healthy' children and complaining they were so stressed because it was nearly Christmas. I rudely told volunteers when they asked if I would give money to a child cancer organisation that I'd just spent $650 on non-Government funded meds for my own child with cancer and he was the only cancer cause I was donating to for now. I'd like to say I became more tolerant and filled with valour, but no. I worked hard to hold it together when I was with my children. I wanted to instil the belief that we could cope with whatever life threw at us but at times my emotions ambushed me. Harry was seated with his class, unaware, but I dashed out of his school Christmas service floundering with an almost comedic combination of uncontrollable sobs, wayward tissues and a door that refused to open. Five minutes later a parent came outside to check because, despite the door being shut, they could still hear my sobs. Gulp!

I feel uneasy when I reflect on how generous people were with gifts, words and food, their time, wisdom and love. The multitude of cards and letters from strangers that I regret we never wrote back to. I will always feel like I never said thank you properly to friends or strangers. A mother of a child in Harry's class who I barely knew at the time regularly sent home gifts and 'I saw this and thought it might make you smile' sentiments. Somehow her thoughtfulness arrived on my worst days. Another friend brought over groceries and cooked when I had exhausted every recipe and Jake couldn't think of a single thing he could stomach. She got about two dozen dumplings into him.

The best support came from those who helped me gain strength. They let me wrestle with my emotions and didn't judge or shy away from it. They kept in very regular contact, and responded in kind; when I cried, they cried; when I laughed, they laughed too; and when I sent texts from the hospital that were simply a string of expletives as yet another worry unfolded, they took colourful language to a whole new level. Some did my thinking for me. I would phone and say 'Tell me what to do, I just can't think'. They would come up with a plan. My colleagues became my work-memory when that disappeared and forgave my flippant cancer one-liners. A former colleague who had been diagnosed with Burkitt's when she was Jake's age made contact. Her insight and humour became invaluable. When Jemima chose to stand beside Jake her actions took my breath away. Jake and Jem are wise beyond their years. I was a little apprehensive meeting Jem's family. What must they think . . . ? How will they be . . . ? Phew, grace and kindness personified.

I've discovered remission is far from the extended party I anticipated it would be when we were in the thick of treatment. Don't get me wrong, it hasn't gone unnoticed that all this could have ended differently — cancer took my Mum and only just spared my son. However the 'party vision' was a bit like a mirage that dried up on arrival (leaving post-party mess and hangover!). There's a whole host of new and unexpected issues to contend with. We have to process what has happened, let go of plans that are no longer feasible, face new health challenges and manage the nagging fear that cancer/death is lurking around our next corner. My brain morphs every pain or fever Jake gets into it being the cancer, that unwelcomed visitor, returning because cancer stole my rational mind.

We will never get 'our old life back' to quote Harry. This is our life. I won't forget Harry sitting on his bed the first school day after remission was announced and crying because he thought life was going to be perfect when his brother's cancer was gone. And although it is much, much better, it isn't perfect. Remission and grief have more in common than I expected.

I read somewhere that up to 30 per cent of fathers and 40 per cent of mothers may exhibit moderate to severe symptoms of post-traumatic stress; similar to that experienced by war veterans and victims of violent crime. I get that. Each day I make a conscious decision not to be in those statistics. I'll do 'whatever it takes'. I'll tackle my fear of Jake's cancer returning and I'll get over the memories. I have experienced the occasional flashback and in particular Jake being wheeled in for a kidney biopsy and shouting that he was dying. I felt completely powerless to save him. Elaine said the way to take the sting out of something painful is to 'talk it to death' — talk until you are bored with it instead of scared or worried. I've got some talking to do.

People say I must want to keep Jake close and wrap him up in cotton wool. I don't. I know close isn't necessarily safe. I believe a person doesn't cheat death only to sit on the couch with their 'olds'. He needs to get the most out of every extra day he has been gifted. I've told him to go and adventure the hell out of life. And to ring regularly with tales of his adventures or there will be trouble!

I am looking forward to more joy and laughter. I know it will be all the sweeter because we have shared such angst. I have had moments like that already. The laughter is heartier. It comes from deeper in my belly — a place carved out by this experience. It lifts me higher than before.

Today, despite being a bit worse for wear, I'm grateful for my deeper connection to Jake, a more meaningful connection to others, and the fact that I never had to walk alone. Well, maybe I did at times, but not for too long. I'm grateful for the subtle shifts in my parenting and for the significant shifts in the way I view the world. The opportunity to refine myself, for my new courage and self-knowledge. I hope I don't lose this me. I don't want to slide back to who I was. I like focusing on the meaningful things and appreciating the smallest of blessings. A person who feels more thankful, relieved, lucky and excited about what tomorrow brings.

After Jem left for Australia, Mum got quite worried that my sadness was sliding into depression. I don't think it was, but my brain had a lot to process. I had two different lives. In one I was head boy of a school, I was going to go to university, I played sports and had loads of mates. Then I got cancer. After the cancer had gone, I had no school, no work, my girlfriend was gone, and a whole lot of people knew who I was. I was looking at my life, seeing a blank canvas and wondering where to start.

Day 114 (day 24 of remission)
Dear Jake

I know you feel sad at the moment. It makes sense. Here is some stuff that may help you. If for no other reason than one day you may have to talk to others about this (thinking about the question the Aussie TV crew asked you about what you would say to others going through difficult times).

Here is a website that might be useful: www.thelowdown.co.nz

I don't know if anything in here may help you, but I was grateful when I was sad that I was able to:
1. Eat and sleep. I always felt worse when I was hangry or tired.
2. Sit with the feelings and not shy away from them. 'Oh look, there I am crying cos I feel sad.' 'That's my heart racing because I'm scared.' 'I am scared this blood clot might be travelling to Jake's lungs and kill him like Jonah Lomu.' 'I feel angry cos this feels so unfair for Jake.' Then I would just sit there feeling it rather than trying to push it down.
3. Reach out for help. I sent lots of texts.
4. Plan one nice thing a day — a coffee with someone or a bunch of flowers in the house.
5. Listen to music that made me feel less alone. Unsurprisingly 'You'll Never Walk Alone' got thrashed a little. As did 'Oh Holy Night' over Xmas. A real gospel version. You'll have your own — probably songs that remind you of happy times with Jem.

6. Look for the small moments of wonder or beauty. One day it was as simple as the view from our house that made me feel less sad. I took a picture of it. Seems ridiculous but at times the little happy moments were all I had and they counted.

7. Stay in the moment — didn't think about how much nicer it was before or how bad it could be in the future. Just dealt with right then, that moment. That hour. Pulled my mind back when it started to get away on me.

8. Remind myself the voice in my head is not my friend. A frenemy at best. My worst enemy at times.

9. Act kindly towards others. This has some weird healing power and lessens pain.

10. Learn about mindfulness. I have a book if you want to read it.

11. Remind myself of how far I had come and how nothing had broken me yet. I made a decision that whatever the future held it wasn't going to break me because I wouldn't bloody let it.

12. Got up out of bed for other people, not for myself. For you, Harry, Matt, Steve, my school staff/students. Some days I wasn't enough of a reason but I had a responsibility to not let others down.

13. Breathe. Easy to forget but breathing deeply directly impacts on your body.

14. Pray. Prayed for strength to get through. Prayed for the outcome I wanted. Often 20 minutes after praying I would feel a calm come over me. Just like taking a Panadol for pain.

15. Thought about people who had it worse (take a look in the paper) or had it worse historically (Auschwitz, etc).

16. Put things that made me smile next to my bed — angel wings, flowers, cards, your wristbands, and especially a note you had written to wish me a happy day.

17. Turn music up really loud in the car and sing, cry and scream, then get out of the vehicle normal when I arrived at the destination.

18. Watch mindless TV.

19. Light a candle.

20. Cry in the shower — magically cleansing.

21. Sweated it out in the gym.

22. Read about people with more courage than me. As you have inspired so many, I also sought out words that would keep me going. I love this poem. It makes me think of you and Elaine:

> **Invictus**
> Out of the night that covers me,
> Black as the pit from pole to pole,
> I thank whatever gods may be
> For my unconquerable soul.

In the fell clutch of circumstance
I have not winced nor cried aloud.
Under the bludgeonings of chance
My head is bloody, but unbowed.

Beyond this place of wrath and tears
Looms but the Horror of the shade,
And yet the menace of the years
Finds, and shall find, me unafraid.

It matters not how strait the gate,
How charged with punishments the scroll,
I am the master of my fate:
I am the captain of my soul.

—William Ernest Henley

I am grateful now that you are in remission. I still worry for you of course and I am always here to talk to. Wake me or call me anytime. You are never alone. Love, Mum xx

I started formulating part of my plan to get my legs working again. This would require firm determination and something new, some different therapies. We discussed what we found on the internet with a neurologist we hadn't met until that point, and he practically had a laughing fit over what he seemed to see as our inherent stupidity. We decided to continue to seek them out anyway.

I started taking a whole lot of natural supplements that a doctor in Mapua, near Nelson, had prescribed for me. He said that they're commonly used in hospitals overseas for patients with chemo nerve damage, but they're not used here yet. I decided that there was no harm in taking them and, let's face it, things couldn't get much worse. Among other things I had to give myself injections of vitamin B_{12} and I was taking vitamin E, folic acid (correctly this time!) and alpha lipoic acid.

I also started having acupuncture. A family friend very generously provided me with a series of treatments at no cost because ACC still hadn't approved my claim. He is seriously skilled, and while I trusted him the needles made me anxious — probably because I'd had a few months of having needles poked in my spine while I was in hospital and the intrathecals are still something I'd rather not experience again. I had to put that fear aside, however, because my legs equalled my freedom and my freedom was hanging in the balance.

The one good thing about that time was that my eyebrows had grown back, and my hair and my eyelashes started to come back, too. Another glimmer of hope was that I managed to do two hours' work at the bar, with a crutch, without it negatively affecting my legs. Maybe, just maybe, those nerves were growing back.

There is no right way to feel during or after treatment. My way and your way might be different but both are valid and appropriate. Some of your emotions may surprise you. Talk to people you trust about how you are feeling. Verbalising it might even help you work out how you are feeling.

If you don't want to talk or think about it, box it up, put it aside and get on with living. In time you may feel like taking the box out and exploring the contents. Or not. If it can stay in the box without tripping you up, then there is nothing to say you actually have to put it under a microscope and relive it all.

16 | LAYING THE FOUNDATIONS

MOTHERS WILL ALWAYS FIND A WAY TO EMBARRASS THEIR SONS

The two weeks between booking our flights and leaving for the Gold Coast went pretty slowly, but eventually the day came around. I couldn't wait to get there and see Jem.

One of the things I learned is that whenever you go out and you have crutches, the first question anyone asks you is, 'What did you do to yourself?' That was always really awkward. At Christchurch Airport, boarding the plane to go on the trip, one of the members of the ground crew said, 'Oh, what have you done to yourself?' Mum turned around and said, 'He got cancer.' I just about died of embarrassment.

Mum and I were sharing a two-bedroom unit in a Gold Coast hotel, and the look on Mum's face when she realised that she'd be spending four nights in the single bed in a little room was absolutely hilarious. Meanwhile, Jem and I had a king-sized bed and an ensuite.

While we were sitting on the balcony enjoying the view over the water, Mum looked at her phone and realised that that day would have been my last day of chemo if I'd had the six rounds I'd been prescribed. I can't imagine how broken I would have been if I'd had to endure another two rounds. I'd still be bald, and I shudder to think what kind of state my legs would have been in. Never mind the fact that I don't know how I would have coped with Jem going away if I'd still been having treatment.

One night, I decided to put my good luck to the test so we went to the casino. I quickly won about $600 — maybe it was true that I'd used up all my bad luck by having cancer! Oh, but then I managed to lose it all again, so maybe my good luck had been used up when my chemo course got cut by a third, and now I'm back in neutral. Jem wasn't very impressed.

DON'T FORGET TO LOOK UP

Being on the Gold Coast was amazing. I was still in awe of the place at the time as there were tall buildings, which

Christchurch doesn't have, and there was warm seawater, which Christchurch definitely doesn't have. Most of all, it had Jem, which was the best thing of all.

I started to contemplate what my life was going to look like when my legs started working properly again. I could really see myself living on the Gold Coast and it felt so good to be thinking about the future at last. Mum and I even checked out possible places for me to live if I moved over to join Jem.

While we were there, we went out to some night markets to eat. I accidentally went out without my crutches and there I was in a bustling night market, and on my own two feet. When I realised what I'd done, I was so excited. Forgetting to take my crutch showed how much my legs were improving although I was absolutely terrified that I was going to fall over. The fear of being embarrassed is universal!

When we left Brisbane, I didn't feel quite so sad to say goodbye to Jem as I thought I would. I was so excited about moving to Australia and I couldn't wait to get back to Christchurch to start planning the move. I think it helped, too, that from then on, when I talked to Jem, I knew I'd be able to picture where she was sitting, I'd know what her place was like, I'd know what her surroundings were like and I'd know the places she was talking about. That made the distance between us so much easier.

There was, however, one small hiccup as I re-entered New Zealand. I handed my arrival card to the Customs officer and couldn't understand why he pulled me aside to 'ask me a couple of questions'. On the line that asks you to list your occupation, I'd written 'public speaker' — that's the work it looked like I was going to be doing after all the offers I had received — and I figured it was less suspicious than saying 'barman' when I couldn't always stand up very well. The only problem was he hadn't read it as 'public speaker', he'd read it as 'public streaker'! Once the misunderstanding was cleared up, I was free to come home.

Coming back to Christchurch, I got the great news that the guy I'd got to know in hospital, who also had Burkitt's, was in remission as well. Other good news came in the form of several more requests for me to do speeches at corporate gigs and schools. I was excited by the prospect of being able to share my story with big groups of people, and equally pleased that I might be able to make some sort of living while doing it. It sure beat the money I was earning in my two-hour shifts at the bar.

But amid all this good news there was still one thing that was niggling at me. On the day we flew back from the Gold Coast, I had a weird sensation in my nose. I was a bit worried about it as it felt a bit like the cancer had felt when it was in my sinuses. I decided I'd get it checked out when I got home. That turned into a bit more of a drama than I expected.

After a few days at home, I started to feel a bit crook. I didn't think about it much, I just wanted to go to bed and sleep until I felt better. However, Mum had other ideas, especially because she knew the last few times

I went to bed sick I'd ended up in hospital.

Given her last sobbing episode getting me through A&E, we agreed that Matt should probably drive me to hospital and that Dad would meet us there. I ended up back in the BMTU for almost a week.

Day 136 (day 46 of remission)
Dear Jake

That is some crazy trick you played on me tonight. There I was looking forward to getting home from a work trip away and boom, you were admitted to hospital overnight. Sorry I overreacted. All I can do is repeat what I said at the time — I simply cannot lose you. Nor can our family. None of us.

I will always feel like I didn't react soon enough last time. Stage four = bad mother. Then Harry needed glasses = bad mother 2/2.

What I know about you is you are brave. So, when you say you feel sick and climb into bed, then the shit really has hit the fan. Without wanting to lecture you, my darling, you will need to learn how to monitor that yourself. Only you know how sick you feel.

Lecture over. For today. Now for some celebration:
1.   Your haematologist being on call when I phoned the hospital (phew).

2. Georgia being at the BMTU when you arrived (according to your dad).
3. Matt said you showed strong fortitude throughout the journey to hospital and into admission.
4. Even though you saw me get a little mental with concern and love for you, before you left for the hospital you gave me a hug and I hope that meant you kinda get that my reactions come from a place of love, deep love for you. If I didn't care, well, that would be a different reaction.
5. Remission.

I love you to the point it cripples me when life isn't going your way . . . no empathy needed because that is just what being a parent is about. You'll have your turn one day.

Love, Mum xx

PS: Take care, darling. Sweet dreams in the BMTU — I wish I'd kept count of the number of nights you have slept there. Will be thinking of you. x

Over the next few days I slowly got back into the rhythm of being in the BMTU. I was neutropenic so I had a room to myself, thank goodness. I was also glad to spend time with some of my favourite nurses, who would come and chat with me when they weren't busy. On the downside, being neutropenic when not on chemotherapy is possibly a sign of a relapse. Bloody hell, just when things had started looking up.

A bunch of blood tests and a CT scan on my sinus area were ordered, and I was put on intravenous antibiotics. I never actually believed it was cancer — and it didn't take long before I was feeling much better, but I still had to stay in hospital until it was completely clear what was going on.

Within a couple of days, my haematologist was able to reassure me that it looked like I had a virus, and not that the lymphoma had reared its ugly head again. The CT scan results came back and, instead of creeping cancer, I had a bog standard sinus infection, probably caught on the plane to Aussie.

I was meant to be giving a speech at Christchurch Boys' on 18 March, but had to postpone it on account of being in hospital. I hoped no one thought the worst when they heard this. At the assembly, I was going to be presented with my award from Massey University for Quote of the Year. Instead, there was a presentation at the hospital, which seemed kind of fitting in some ways.

While I was in hospital, one of my favourite nurses, Kat, was fundraising for Shave for a Cure. She spends her working life helping patients with cancer treatment, and then decides to shave off her hair to fundraise for Leukaemia and Blood Cancer New Zealand. Amazing. That just goes to prove the quality of the people I had looking after me in the BMTU.

Five days in and I was feeling heaps better, but for

some reason my neutrophil levels weren't climbing as much as they were supposed to. I had to stay in hospital until they did, or until I had a bone marrow biopsy to make sure I was clear of lymphoma.

On day 51 of my remission, I was allowed to go home for the night, but had to be back first thing the next morning. By this stage I'd had four injections of G-CSF, a drug that stimulates your bone marrow to produce blood cells, so my neutrophils had improved slightly.

HEARING UNEXPECTED THINGS DOESN'T ALWAYS MEAN YOU'RE HALLUCINATING

A couple of days later, I was back visiting hospital for another bone marrow biopsy to make sure the lymphoma hadn't returned.

Before the biopsy, I said to one of the nurses, 'Do you think you could get me some happy drugs to help me through this one?' She told me she'd check with the doctors. I'd already tried lorazepam, clonazepam and diazepam, and none of them had really worked for me when it came to lumbar punctures. She talked to the doctors and came back with good news. 'They're going to give you midazolam this time.'

Midazolam is one of the strongest sedatives you can get. I took the tiny white pill while I was watching TV in my room. The next thing I remember, I was lying on the floor of my room naked, using my hospital gown as a blanket to keep myself warm. One of the nurses, Shoko, was standing above me, saying, 'Jake? Jake? Are you okay?' I came to and said, 'Yeah, yeah, I'm fine' as I dragged myself back into bed and tried to finish putting my gown on, only to be utterly confounded by trying to tie it closed.

I then went in and had the procedure where they gave me a general anaesthetic before taking a sample of bone marrow and a sliver of bone.

I was lying in bed after the procedure and I swear I could hear someone playing guitar and singing to me. Afterwards I concluded I must have been so high that I was hallucinating. I also decided I was going to take my own IV line out, for some reason. So I lay there and ripped my line out and sprayed blood all over the place.

Took midazolam, got naked, lay on the floor, hallucinated music and ripped my IV line out. Just another normal day in the BMTU! Thankfully, the preliminary results came through quickly, showing no sign of cancer, so I got to go home that night.

About two weeks later, I was watching *Seven Sharp* and who should I see but Dr Sean MacPherson, who was one of the haematologists from Christchurch Hospital. They call him The Singing Haematologist because he does some of his lectures in musical form. And there he was, sitting in a hospital room — which just happened to have been next door to my one — playing guitar and singing. I hadn't been hallucinating after all!

One thing that might sound like I hallucinated it, but which is absolutely true, came to light when Mum got a phone call a couple of days later. She came into my room and woke me up, looking worried and a bit confused, 'I've just been on the phone to the police.'

I momentarily wondered what I'd done that would mean the police were looking for me, and that I wouldn't want Mum to know about. The real story was way weirder than anything I could possibly have done.

Mum explained: 'The police got in touch because there's a 24-year-old woman from Turkey who has watched your videos and she's obsessed with you.'

Weird. But wait, there's more.

'She has come into the country with the sole purpose of finding you and marrying you.'

WHAT? I really thought Mum was joking. That couldn't possibly be real, could it? Mum and I had a few jokes about dowry and Turkish Delight, but it was way more serious than I initially thought.

It turned out that the people she was staying with, and who were sponsoring her, were so concerned for my safety that they went to the police to tell them. She had done so much research that she knew where Mum worked, she even thought she knew where we lived — but, thankfully, we'd moved house. She had told people that she was going to marry me and would stop at nothing to make it happen. That was quite scary.

For quite a while after that I never went anywhere by myself, and when I was in public places I was always on high alert. I constantly checked to make sure no one was following me. The police were tracking her and monitoring her movements, and were in communication with Immigration about her status. Eventually, she went back to Turkey of her own accord — and I remain unmarried. Thank goodness.

FIND WAYS TO MEASURE HOW FAR YOU'VE COME

Thankfully, my Turkish stalker didn't put me off going to the airport as Jem arrived home in the wee hours of Easter Sunday. I was so happy to see her and we made the most of her time back in Christchurch.

While Jem was home, I got the great (and expected) news that my bone marrow biopsy was completely clear and that I'd gone neutropenic as a result of the virus I had. Knowing that meant I was able to set some short-term goals again, and also to start thinking about life in the longer term. One of these goals was to spend Jem and my six-month anniversary together on the Gold Coast on 9 April, which was only a couple of weeks away.

My ability to set bigger goals was aided by the fact that my legs had finally started getting better. I slowly went from needing two crutches, to having one crutch in the house and two while I was out in public. Then I went down to having one crutch all the time — at home and in public. That was a big win for me.

Then, one day, I woke up in the morning and went to make myself breakfast. When I was in the kitchen, toasting some muffins, I realised I'd left my crutch in the bedroom. I'd walked all the way from my bedroom to the kitchen on my own without even realising!

After that it became a real battle. I stopped using a crutch inside but was still using one when I went out in public. I would think 'How much can I stretch this?'

The nerve damage had been so bad that I was enrolled at the Burwood Spinal Unit, the country's biggest specialist back and neck rehabilitation centre. I was doing the sort of rehab that people who have broken their backs do — things like walking while hanging onto parallel bars. They basically had to teach me how to walk again.

I'd go out to Burwood once a week and the physio would test my progress. They'd measure how long I could stand on both feet without holding onto anything, or how long I could balance on one foot. When I first started, I could balance on one foot with my eyes open for about two seconds. I then had to progress to doing that with my eyes closed.

One day I went in there and the physio asked me how long I could stand on both feet with my eyes closed. I stood there while she timed me. I got to a minute and a half and she said, 'I think I'll just stop you there.'

It was great that they measured my progress every week because I could see that I was gradually getting better. It was hard to gauge otherwise because at different times of the day my legs would feel better or worse depending on what I'd been doing. When I got to the point that I didn't need a crutch to go out in public anymore, that was amazing.

For months afterwards, I'd get up in the morning and, if I needed to go somewhere, I'd walk there, and I'd think 'Way to go, this is fantastic! I love that I can walk!' I was always offering to go to the supermarket to get things just because I could walk. I'd be like, 'I can walk to the supermarket. I can even walk around the supermarket. I'm so fancy! Have you seen how well my legs work?' I loved it.

EMBRACE EACH DAY

Ten days after Jem had come home for Easter, I was jumping on a plane to go and see her in Australia. Before I left, I had my neutrophil levels checked to make sure my immune system was up to travelling. Thankfully, the doctors gave me the nod, and Mum was up early to take me to the airport. Heading over there this time was different as I knew exactly where I was going, and I knew that one day soon I'd be living on the Gold Coast, too.

The week with Jem flew by as we celebrated our six-month anniversary and planned for me to spend more time at Surfers Paradise during the year. Some people might see celebrating a six-month anniversary as a bit silly, but given we didn't know if I'd ever make it to see that milestone, it felt to us like a day worth making a fuss of. I'm still blown away by the way Jem stood by me when I first got sick, and the way she's continued to fight in my corner ever since. One of the things I'm most grateful to the cancer for is the way that it has strengthened our relationship.

Our anniversary was just one example of my firm belief in the need to embrace every single day. I know everyone's heard all sorts of clichés about life being a precious gift and how you should live life to the fullest. I always hated them, too. But now I realise that was because I never realised how fragile life really is.

Before I got sick I was always dying to get home and watch TV, dying for the weekend, dying for the school hoidays . . . until I was actually dying in Christchurch Hospital. I could never have imagined it, pictured it, or believed it could happen until it actually did. And now I know for sure that it is vitally important to make the most of life while you can.

17 | MY CHALLENGE TO ALL OF US

Coming home from Australia, I had a pretty firm plan of how the next few months were going to look. Jem and I spent plenty of time talking about what I would do and how we could maximise our time together. Having come through my latest medical setback, I was ready to commit to some of the new opportunities that had come my way as a result of my speech back in November. I was in quite big demand as a public speaker, which meant I was finally able to base myself on the Gold Coast but fly back to New Zealand for events when I needed to. Even then, it was pretty hard being away from Jem for a week or two at a time.

At this stage I was travelling quite a bit — three or four flights per week on average — but hadn't yet qualified for any benefits as a frequent flyer. To alleviate this problem, I perfected the art of standing outside the airport lounge and begging the kindest-looking passengers heading inside to take me in as their 'plus one'. After the generosity I had experienced over the previous year, I had faith in the goodness of people, and my faith was duly rewarded, given I was only turned down once!

Around this time, I was honoured to be asked to come on board as an ambassador for the Māia Health Foundation, a charity with a mission to enhance health services in Canterbury, alongside cricketer Brendon McCullum and singer Bic Runga. It's a cause I'm hugely passionate about, and being able to assist in the incredible work that the Foundation is doing brings me heaps of satisfaction.

LIVE DAY TO DAY

Going back to CBHS and making the speech I'd had to cancel when I was in hospital was great. It made me realise just how far I'd come since I'd last spoken at school. The school had been such a huge part of my life and had been such a support to me when I was sick that it really felt like going home.

Here's a small part of what I said that day:

I'm guessing since I beat cancer that I'm now expected to be able to dish out some serious life advice. I'm not sure I can, but I'll give it a shot.

The most important thing having cancer has done for me is to teach me to live day to day. This is a phrase I used to hate because I didn't understand it. I always liked to plan far ahead, always had a five-year plan for myself and where I wanted to be. This held me in good stead, and I always saw it as a strength of mine. I'm not saying it's a bad thing at all, I don't want to put the guidance counsellor out of a job.

Going through this experience has really taught me how to take things a day at a time, focus on short-term goals and just get through each day. If at the start of this process I had realised what lay ahead of me — the 100 days of chemo and terrible procedures that were in store — it would have seemed impossible to conquer. By putting my energy into just getting through today's chemo, and ignoring the fact there was more to come tomorrow, and the day after, and the day after that, it made it bearable.

Taking everything day by day lets you focus on the now and appreciate life. Tied in with that is the ability to find little bits of light in the darkness, something to focus on to help you get through, and to appreciate the little things. Sometimes they're all you have left.

'Yes, I might have a spinal injection of chemo today, but something good is on TV tonight.' 'Yes, I might have my head in a bucket right now, but I'll probably never feel this sick again in my life.' 'No, I can't go out and live a normal life like everyone else my age is right now, but my girlfriend is bringing in a DVD for us to watch together later.'

Once you can learn to enjoy the little things like this so much, you can't begin to imagine how amazing the big things in life feel! It's something I remind myself of each day, and it makes every day that little bit better.

Live each day with passion and pride, to the very fullest, because you are able to. Every morning that I wake up I know that I'm on borrowed time — every day that I live is another one longer than I was meant to, had my body had its own way. It spurs me on.

MAKE THE MOST OF EVERY OPPORTUNITY THAT COMES YOUR WAY

Over the next few months, I was blessed with some amazing opportunities to speak to groups about my experience with cancer. As well as numerous school groups, I was invited to speak at a couple of important medical conferences — one called 'Powering Up Our Future' was a health symposium looking at ways the medical profession can do things differently, and one was a conference of haematologists.

I felt really lucky to have been given an opportunity to speak directly to the people who will be making the decisions for young people like me who end up in hospital. After one of those speeches, I even got to have a chat with

Chai Chuah, the Director-General of Health for New Zealand. I relished every opportunity I got to praise the medical professionals who had worked with me and to suggest ways in which things could be improved. How many 18-year-olds ever get the chance to do something like that?

While I was in Wellington speaking to health professionals, Mum was celebrating a six-month anniversary of her own.

Day 172 (day 82 of remission)
Dear Jake

What a crazy few months. On Thursday, 22 October 2015 you ended up in hospital for 50 days straight. Tomorrow is Thursday, 21 April so it feels like a six-month anniversary of sorts.

Here's a semi-review of a few of the stages over the last six months:
1. Getting cancer.
2. Getting diagnosed.
3. Getting famous via a viral speech.
4. Getting through endless hours in hospital together.
5. Getting in the paper.
6. Getting through the dumb comments people made.
7. Getting stalked.

8. Getting dressed when Matt was in charge of the washing.
9. Getting life back.
10. Getting back in the media (gotta love these headlines).
11. Getting back on your feet.
12. Getting stalked again.
13. Getting speaking engagements.
14. Getting to Australia.
15. Getting in touch while you are out of town.

Love you completely and forever. Mum xx

PS: Grateful to have had you keep me company through all of the above and that you lived to tell the tale (to many at that).

While Mum's email made the previous six months sound like a whirlwind, the next six months really were one. I was constantly on the move between Australia and New Zealand, switching between relaxing on the beach and giving keynote speeches during the Kiwi winter. It was a strange way to live but it was exciting and unpredictable, and I was determined to make the most of every day.

ALWAYS TAKE THE OPPORTUNITY TO SAY THANK YOU

The Tour de Cure Snow Ball speech in Sydney in June was a really significant one for me. It was my first big speaking engagement in Australia and it was for a cause that was really close to my heart. Tour de Cure is an Australian cancer charity that organises several cycling tours every year to raise funds for cancer research. In the 10 years they've been operating, they've funded 252 cancer research, support and prevention projects to the tune of AU$25 million. I've since come on board as an ambassador for the charity, and I'm hugely excited about the incredible work they do and the amazing progress they're making in cancer research.

Thankfully, I didn't have to get on a bike (yet) as the Snow Ball was a lavish, lycra-free event at The Star in Sydney. As the name suggests, the whole place was decked out like a winter wonderland. It was so glamorous! I doubt I'll have many more opportunities to share the stage with anyone as famous as Melody Thornton (formerly of The Pussycat Dolls).

It was great to be able to talk to the charity's benefactors about how what they do directly affects people like me:

None of you could have prevented me getting cancer; none of you could have saved me from it. You couldn't be there to rub my back while I vomited in my bed; or made my parents feel okay about watching their son dying a little more each day, tiptoeing closer to the edge of that cliff before being swept away from it just in time by modern medicine.

But what you're doing tonight is raising money for researching for a cure, and that's more important than anything you could have done for me. The progress being made is so far beyond me — but I am partly a testament to it. Only 25 years ago Burkitt's was not treatable. That means that 25 years ago, or 9000 days ago, within the lifespan of most of you, if I had have been diagnosed with Burkitt's then I would have died. I would have been a hopeless case, my family would have had to sit around and watch — maybe I would have helped plan my own funeral, at age 18.

That is the power of the research you are funding tonight. But that incredible progress is not a reason to stop now either. I am not out of the woods yet, nor will I ever be really. I could still die from cancer. And so could you — in fact, many of you will, statistically speaking. We, you and I, need events like tonight to save ourselves. That is the power of what you are doing tonight, and you should feel fantastic about it.

NOT ALL ATTENTION IS GOOD ATTENTION

Something I said must have resonated with someone because not only did the charity raise $1.3 million that night, but I ended up with a whole lot more media attention after the event. I didn't mind it most of the time but there was the odd time when things went too far.

After one speech I made in Auckland, I was staying at a hotel in the central city. I was quite tired and I wasn't feeling up to doing any media interviews so I declined a couple of requests. Consequently, one of the TV stations knew where I was staying and they got a camera team to stake out the hotel. I was told that as soon as I stepped outside and off private property, they were within their rights to photograph me. I couldn't go outside because a major media organisation was stalking me. It was completely insane, but it did make for some good laughs as well.

TOO MUCH OF A GOOD THING DEPENDS ON THE THING

Moving overseas has been a good thing for me and my family. We all really miss each other but we'd spent so much time together while I was in hospital, that, to be fair, we got pretty sick of each other. That said, in my life over the past year, there are two things that have remained constant throughout everything — my family and my girlfriend. I might not physically be with my family all the time, but I know that they are right there beside me and support me.

Even though we weren't living in the same place any-more, I decided to heed some of Mum's advice when I moved to Australia. In an email in early January, she outlined the top 10 things research says I should do in order to remain cancer-free after chemotherapy. They were:

1. Don't smoke.
2. Stay lean.
3. Limit consumption of red meat. Replace with fish, eggs or vegetable proteins.
4. Eat more fruits, vegetables and legumes, as well as foods based on whole grains.
5. Exercise regularly.
6. Limit daily alcohol to two glasses per day for men (one for women).
7. Limit salt and products containing salt, like chips, or those preserved in salt.
8. Don't get sunburnt.
9. Use good food rather than supplements.
10. Cancer survivors should follow the above to the letter.

Okay, that's only nine things, but she was under a bit of stress at the time!

Adopting a much healthier lifestyle than I had before I got sick has been pretty easy. A lot of people think of the Gold Coast as a real party place, but I hardly ever go out. My life has been very stable and sensible.

Jem is very focused on her studies — she's working toward a Bachelor of Business degree — and is also a dedicated member of her university track team. As an élite athlete, she doesn't drink and she needs a lot of sleep.

It probably also helps that none of my mates from back home live here! When I come back to New Zealand, I'll go out, but I don't really drink anymore — it's just not a factor in my life now. Besides, I quite enjoy sending them Snapchats of me on the beach while they're sitting in lectures!

TREAT YOUR BODY WELL

I started eating really healthy food to try to get my body back into balance. Dinner might be five different vegetables in a stir-fry with lean meat plus I eat heaps of tropical fruit every day, which is easy to do as it's so delicious.

I've never treated my body so well in my life — it's pretty much the opposite of how I treated it before I got sick. I took my health for granted then. Now, I feel like my body just needs the good stuff and I'm learning to listen to it.

18 | THE FUTURE IS TRULY IN OUR HANDS

WORRY HAS ITS PLACE

Every time I get sick or my body does something weird, I worry a bit that I might be relapsing. I've had a couple of scares including a couple of big ones since I've been in Aussie. One was when I found a lump under my arm. I couldn't think of any other way to explain it — I was sure I had cancer again. I didn't.

Another time I started getting pain in my jaw. It was exactly the same kind of pain as I'd experienced before

I was diagnosed and it was in exactly the same place. I went into A&E and had a CT scan. It was negative. I later found out the pain was because I'd been grinding my teeth while I was sleeping!

It's really hard to turn that thought process off. Any unusual feeling or pain in my body and I go straight to wondering if I'm relapsing.

I met a woman once whose husband had had lymphoma. He'd found the lump under his arm while they were out driving. She told me that whenever they got in the car to go for a drive, he would feel under his arm, checking for lumps. When she pointed this out to him, he had no idea he was even doing it. It was a completely subconscious thing. I get that because I do things like that, too.

MAKE THE STATISTICS WORK FOR YOU

Luckily for me, lymphoma has a five-year timeframe — unlike some other cancers where it's about 15 years. Your statistical likelihood of relapsing decreases at six months, one year, two years and five years. I've gone past the six-month one, which was around the time I had pain in my jaw, and the one-year one, so things are looking good.

The five-year survival rate is almost 60 per cent, which doesn't take into account the people who die straight away.

My odds are slightly worse than some Burkitt's survivors because the cancer reached my brain. I also didn't finish all my intrathecal treatment, and we don't know for sure whether the four rounds administered — because I was treated as an adult — were sufficient compared to the six rounds given to paediatric patients. When you look at it, I was only a few months from qualifying as paediatric. My haematologist reckoned there was about a one in three to a one in four chance of the cancer coming back. That sounds like a lot until you flip it around — there's a 66 to 75 per cent chance that it won't come back!

Some people find that upsetting, but it's just what I live with. The knowledge of it makes me much more proactive about looking after myself. If I feel like anything might be wrong, I go straight to the doctor now. I don't take any chances with my health.

It changes the way I look at life, too. I could be back in hospital in Christchurch having chemo again within days, instead of living the life I want with Jem on the Gold Coast. Approaching life like that means I also treat the most important people in my life as well as I can. I spend every day that I get doing exactly what I want and as much of it as I want because I know my days might still be limited.

I'm not prepared to die knowing I've done things I didn't want to do, or that I hadn't done things I wanted to do. That's especially the case because I've had a warning that I could die. Now that I've had the warning shot fired, I have to do everything that I can to make the most of every day, just in case the cancer does come back and I die from it.

It's a case of prepare for the worst and hope for the

best. By doing that, the cancer doesn't play on my mind at all. I don't resent it. It doesn't make me worry or keep me awake at night. It works as a really awesome motivation to get stuff done and I'm grateful for that. I don't see cancer as a thief, I see it as giving me the focus to do the things in life that I want to do.

NOW IS GOOD

People live life with the idea 'I don't need to do it now, I've got plenty of time.' Most of the time that's true — but not always. And now it's a race for me to see how many people I can move, how many lives I can change, how many cities I can visit, how many flights I can take, how much new ground I can break, and how many things I can do that most 19-year-olds don't get a chance to do, before I die. Then, when I do die, I'll die with a legacy, and that gives me peace.

When I die, whenever that may be, I am determined to have created something that lives on. I've donated a trophy for gallantry to Christchurch Boy's High, my winning quote is going up on the wall there; there'll be people who remember meeting me, there'll be people who remember listening to my speech. When I die, I'll know that I've given my best shot at leaving the world a slightly better place through my actions. People have told me my words have helped them hang on when they came close to letting go.

Of course, I'd prefer not to die before my time. I'd rather keep doing my thing, and I'd be really sad for my family and for my girlfriend, but my position is that dying is not something for me to worry about. I'm not scared of dying. After all, I'm not the one that has to clean up the mess that would be left if I did die. One of the main reasons I take such good care of myself is because I feel I owe it to my loved ones. If the cancer did come back and I hadn't looked after myself, that would have been unfair on all of the people who have cared for me so well.

Every day that I get is another one longer than I might have had. Every morning when I wake up, I know that I'm on borrowed time. It makes me feel a little insecure and uneasy, but I am so grateful for it. Waking up every day knowing that if your body had its way you would have been dead is a pretty uncomfortable feeling. I know that I'm only alive because of medicine and a hell of a lot of luck — and I might not be this time next year. I think about it whenever I'm booking flights to go somewhere — I think, 'I wonder if my cancer will have come back by then? I wonder if I'll be alive then?' I guess that's true for everyone to some degree, but I don't think anyone really lives with that ever-present possibility until they come close to death.

It's a bit morbid to constantly be thinking about dying, but it does its job in that it makes me focus on living. If you start your day with the outlook of it being another day that you're lucky to have, very little can go wrong. I know it's frustrating to the people around me when they get upset about little things and I'm quite blasé about it. It's just that it's hard for me to get wound up about something that's not life-or-death. The core of it comes down to the fact that anything this side of death is manageable. It might be difficult, it could be uncomfortable, but it can be dealt with.

LIFE ISN'T GOING TO BE EASY — FOR ANYONE

If life isn't difficult, then check your pulse, you may be dead already. Everyone I know has their own challenges. Social media and television may fool us into believing that we deserve a perfect life, and that anything less means we've been short-changed. That is not the reality. Life has no smooth road for any of us. What matters is our ability to bounce back from adversity — some people are crushed by misfortune, and others grow from it.

Your perception will influence your experience of the inevitable challenges you will have to face. A phrase my nana, Elaine, imprinted on me was: 'Is it as bad as Auschwitz?' Without exception, the answer is always no. Was me getting cancer as bad as Auschwitz? No, it wasn't. Is your car breaking down as bad as Auschwitz? No, it's not. Is anything that might happen to you in your lifetime as bad as Auschwitz? Probably not. It's a sobering way to keep things in perspective.

MARK THE MILESTONES

A year after my diagnosis, I spoke at the 2016 prizegiving at my old school. I felt like that was the end of the story in some ways. I'm not 'Cancer Boy' anymore. I don't want to be harping on about this period in my life for longer than anyone wants to hear about it. I am going to have to work hard not to have that tiny part of my life define the whole of it. Some people get their lives defined for them by short periods of time when they do something stupid — thankfully that wasn't the case for me.

My story is not that I had cancer when I was 18, it's what I've done since. The more people I get to meet and the more of life I see, the less relevant my cancer becomes to my overall story. I know now that I'm not grateful for life just because I nearly died, but because in the process of nearly dying I met people who did die. I met children who needed three years of chemo. I met people who had their lives destroyed. I learnt that I wasn't unlucky to get cancer, I was lucky to not have something worse happen to me.

Some anniversaries to do with my cancer stick out for me well ahead of the date — probably about half of them. Others, though, slip past without me even noting them until a few days after. I'm not sure which is nicer — the recognition of the dates is special, but if I do forget them, then so is the knowledge that life is rolling on regardless.

End-of-year speech, CBHS

I'm pretty thrilled about how different the speech I'm about to make is from the one I did this time last year. The last time I made a speech on this stage, I didn't know if I would live to see this school ever again. I vividly remember, as my dad wheeled me back out to the car to go back to hospital and I was vomiting into a sick bucket, Mr Bone coming out to hold the door for us. I will never forget the look on his face, which I read as him not knowing if he would ever see me again. And I definitely was wondering if I would ever see him again. I remember looking back over my shoulder to the audience as Dad wheeled me off stage, trying to spot a familiar face or a friend, in case that was the last time I ever saw them.

The first three weeks of my treatment were critical as the aggressive chemo regime attacked the aggressive cancer and my kidneys were caught in the crossfire. It was day three of chemotherapy when I made that speech, and the cancer had the upper hand on me. At that stage, my body was failing me more every day.

But, fortunately, none of that matters anymore. Not the statistics, or the chances, or the memories, however much they may hurt. Because I'm still here today, 364 days on, to speak to you tonight, and I am absolutely honoured, and privileged, to do so. It's also quite nice to be standing rather than in a wheelchair, although I may have recycled the sign from last year saving me a carpark.

My life now is perhaps slightly more settled, but unchanged in the sense of how completely different it is to anything that I would have ever imagined at the start of last year — yet another case of something I couldn't ever imagine happening, a recurring theme over the past 12 months, it seems.

Right now I'm based on the Gold Coast full-time with my girlfriend, and it works as a great base for me to do public speaking across New Zealand and Australia. The environment is everything my body needs as I recover — low stress, relaxed and warm. I've signed a book deal and worked hard on a documentary, which will come out next year. It's been a busy year, an exciting year, but above all a year of my life that I'm just grateful to have had. And I know there's only more to come next year.

I'm back tonight to present a new award, which the school has honoured me by allowing me to donate. Tonight I will, for the first time, present the Jake Bailey Cup for Gallantry — for great courage, strength and resilience in the face of adversity. In a lot of ways, it is for moral strength, something which I eerily talked about last time I was on this stage. I said, 'We can't all be the best scholar achieving straight excellences or the best sportsman in the first XV, believe me. While we can't be the best at everything or even, at times, even anything, what we can choose is to have moral strength. Moral strength is about making a conscious decision to be a person who doesn't give up when it would be easy to. To be lesser because the journey is less arduous.'

I want the moral of this award, and my story, to be that when a terrible thing happens, you have the choice to let it cripple you, or to make you stronger. This award recognises those who stare down adversity, and then use it as motivation to push themselves forward. Those who know that bravery isn't when you don't feel fear, or pain, or sadness, but to have the ability to feel them and move forward anyway. General George Patton once said, 'I don't measure a man's success by how high he climbs, but by how high he bounces when he falls.' This award is for those who have dropped, and then bounced high with their resilience, courage and gallantry. I have discussed the inaugural winner of the award with Mr Hill and the thing that stands out about this student is that he has very strong principles and that he sticks to them.

So, to the Year 13 leavers — I wish you all the best as you set sail from the port where you've been docked for the past five years. May you venture far and wide, always with an association to this mighty institution. To the Year 12s who have been selected as monitors — congratulations, and welcome to a team of incredible men who will forever leave a mark on you. And to whoever out there is to be selected as Senior Monitor for 2017, I'll give you the same advice I gave Jake 3.0: don't drink Diesels, and don't get cancer.

Whatever you think of Lance Armstrong, the following quote from him really resonated with me: 'The truth is cancer is the best thing that ever happened to me. I don't know why I got the illness but it did wonders for me and I wouldn't walk away from it. Why would I want to change for even a day the most important and shaping event in my life?'

I completely get that. I wouldn't change anything that happened to me. It's nothing to do with the speech or being recognised or any of the things that have come into my path as a result. It's about what it taught me. What I learned about life, what I learned about death, and what I learned about myself.

Going through a few really terrible months has set me up for the rest of my life, and my mindset is so different to what it would have been otherwise. I've sacrificed those three or four months in order to enjoy the rest of my life so much more. But it has completely changed my view of the world for the better and how I live day to day. Before, I was searching for something distant. Now, I'm in the present.

Once I wanted a corporate job in finance. While I still strive for greater things, I don't want to strive for power or pleasure. I genuinely want to help others overcome their challenges. I have been given an opportunity to turn some of the cancer 'mess' into a 'message'. A *problitunity*. I want to make the most of it.

I'm certainly not suggesting I am more selfless or more altruistic than others. I'm not. What I am doing is reciprocal. When people tell me I have helped them find courage or peace I am truly surprised and humbled, but it also gives me a sense of purpose and it gives my life meaning. It helps me carve out that legacy I'm determined to leave behind.

Thanks cancer, for these unexpected gifts.

I don't know where it goes from here for any of us. For you. And sure as hell not for me. But I wish you the very best in your journey, and I thank you for reading about mine.

GLOSSARY

BIOPSY

During a biopsy, a small sample of tissue is taken so it can be examined for disease. This is usually done by inserting a long, thin needle into the part of the body that is being checked.

BMTU

The Bone Marrow Transplant Unit. The BMTU at Christchurch Hospital not only looks after people having bone marrow transplants but also people who have blood cancers, like lymphoma, leukaemia and myeloma.

BONE MARROW ASPIRATE

Otherwise known as a bone marrow aspiration, this involves sticking a needle into a large bone to remove a small sample of bone marrow. This can then be tested to check whether there is any cancer present. Bone marrow contains cells that produce both white and red blood cells and platelets, low levels of which are a strong indicator of the presence of cancer.

BURKITT'S NON-HODGKIN'S LYMPHOMA

Named after Dennis Burkitt, a doctor who first identified this form of lymphoma in 1958 after seeing it in young people in Africa.

This is a type of cancer that originates in the lymphatic system, which is itself a part of the body's immune system. The lymphatic system helps clean the body of bacteria, viruses and other harmful toxins. It does this by transporting lymph around the body. Lymph is a fluid that contains white blood cells, which fight infection.

All types of lymphoma are classified as non-Hodgkin's, except the ones where a specific abnormal cell (called a Reed-Sternberg cell) is present. If that cell is detected, then the lymphoma is defined as being Hodgkin's.

CANCER

Normal body cells grow and divide, then stop growing and eventually die. Cancer cells grow and divide, but they don't stop growing and they don't die — they just keep going until they're out of control. After a while, these cells clump together to form tumours, which then destroy the normal cells nearby. If left untreated, these tumours can damage the healthy tissue around them, making a person sick. Sometimes cells from the original tumour can travel to other parts of the body and start new tumours, which are known as secondary tumours.

CANCER STAGES

Many cancer diagnoses have a stage number between one and four attached to them. One is the least serious and four is the most serious. These stages are usually thought to mean:

- Stage One: The cancer is relatively small and found only in the site where it started.
- Stage Two: The cancer is a bit bigger, but hasn't spread into the surrounding tissue.
- Stage Three: The cancer is larger and may have started to spread into surrounding tissue.
- Stage Four: The cancer has spread from where it started into other organs of the body. In the case of lymphoma, stage four means that the cancer has spread out of the lymph nodes, for example, to the bone marrow, kidneys or central nervous system.

CHEMOTHERAPY

One of the main ways to treat cancer, chemotherapy involves putting chemicals into the body that stop the cancer cells from splitting and growing. These chemicals are really strong so they can kill other cells as well, which is why some people have side-effects like losing their hair.

There are three main ways that the drugs are administered — directly into the bloodstream by an injection, or an infusion which may run over several hours, through an injection under the skin or by taking tablets or pills.

CT SCAN

CT scans are also sometimes known as CAT scans, which stands for computerised (axial) tomography scans. Basically, a CT scan is a whole lot of x-rays taken from different angles. These are all put together by a computer to give a detailed picture of the inside of your body. The cross-sections that a CT scan produces give an accurate picture of the location and size of any tumours.

HAEMATOLOGIST

A haematologist is a doctor who specialises in diagnosing and treating diseases that are found in blood.

INTRATHECAL INJECTION

This is when drugs are injected straight into the fluid which surrounds the brain and spinal cord. These injections are often used when the medicine needs to get into the brain.

LEUKAEMIA

Leukaemia is a cancer of the blood or bone marrow.

LUMBAR PUNCTURE

This is a lot like an intrathecal injection but instead of putting drugs in, it involves taking fluid out of the spinal cord so it can be examined for diseases.

MAXILLOFACIAL SURGEON

A surgeon who specialises in operating on the jaws and the face.

MRI

MRI scans — otherwise known as magnetic resonance imaging scans — combine magnetism and radio waves to make up a picture of the inside of the body. From looking at the scans, doctors can sometimes tell whether a tumour is cancerous or not. They can also see how far a tumour has spread.

NEUTROPENIC

When someone having chemotherapy is neutropenic, it means that they have very low levels of neutrophils (see below). When someone is neutropenic, if they are exposed to any kind of infection their body will be unable to fight it and they will be at risk of getting very sick.

NEUTROPHILS

Neutrophils are a type of white blood cell that help the body fight infection. They are made in the bone marrow, which is inside the large bones in the body.

PET SCAN

A positron emission tomography scan involves injecting dye that contains radioactive tracers into your bloodstream. This is then absorbed into your body and goes straight to anything that is growing, such as tumours.

PICC LINE

Peripherally inserted central catheter — a tube that gets put into a vein in your arm and is then guided through your body using a wire until it reaches your heart.

REMISSION

When tests and scans show that all signs of cancer have gone, it is called remission. This doesn't mean the person is completely cured, as it can be very difficult to tell whether all of the cancer cells are entirely gone.

ULTRASOUND

During an ultrasound, high-frequency sound waves are aimed at your internal organs. These will echo differently when they are bounced off abnormal tissues, like tumours.

ACKNOWLEDGEMENTS

Despite what a cliché it is, there are genuinely too many people to acknowledge to mention them all by name. People's support and kindness have been the defining factor of my journey and story. From the people I've met to those I never met but made contact with — and to those who have always been there for me — there are many thousands of people to whom I owe my gratitude.

Everyone who has played a part in my story will know they have done so. Every person who has dropped off food, or a card, or sent an email, or a gift, or said a kind word, or given me guidance, or saved my life, or just been there for me and those close to me, will know what they have done. And that makes this your story as well. Thank you so much for your support. It is beyond impossible to repay, but I hope you can imagine what it has meant to me.

Thank you to Nicola and the Penguin Random House New Zealand team for making this dream of mine come true. Without you I would never have been able to share my story with others.